China's Soil Pollution and Degradation Problems

China's air pollution is infamous. The haze can make it impossible to see buildings across the street, and the pollution forces schools to close and creates health and morbidity problems, in addition to tremendous environmental degradation. However, China also faces another important environmental problem, which is less well-known to the public: that of soil degradation and pollution. This book provides an overview of the problems related to soil degradation and pollution throughout China, examining how and why current policy has fallen short of expectation. It also examines the challenges faced by policy makers as they attempt to adopt sustainable practices alongside a booming and ever-expanding economy.

China's Soil Pollution and Degradation Problems utilizes grey literature such as newspaper articles, NGO reports and Chinese government information alongside academic studies in order to provide an extensive review of the challenges faced by grassroots organizations as they tackle environmental policy failings throughout China.

This book will be of great interest to students of environmental pollution and contemporary Chinese studies looking for an introduction to the topics of soil pollution and soil degradation, and for researchers looking for an extensive list of sources and analysis of China's environmental problems more broadly.

Claudio O. Delang is Assistant Professor in the Department of Geography at Hong Kong Baptist University, Hong Kong.

"Official information about the conditions of China's soils has until recently been highly restricted. However, a considerable amount of research has been carried out over the last few years. This book provides a state of the art overview of currently available information, which reveals the dire soil conditions in several parts of China. It is essential reading for all those interested in the subject, and is an important resource for both teaching and research."

— Prof. Bernhart Owen, Department of Geography,
Hong Kong Baptist University, Hong Kong

"After years of neglect, soil degradation and pollution have become serious problems in China. Research on the topic has been growing over the last few years, but due to official secrecy there are no nationwide data, and most information is limited to isolated case studies. This book answers the need for the consolidation of the numerous case studies. It provides a clear review of the existing state of knowledge, and is essential reading for students, practitioners and researchers alike."

— Prof. Lu Xixi, Department of Geography,
National University of Singapore, Singapore

"This book is very timely given the importance of soils to society. It utilises a variety of sources to provide an excellent overview of the soil resources of China. This book will appeal to those with an interest in soils, natural resources, the environment and China."

— Prof. Mervyn R. Peart, Department of Geography,
University of Hong Kong, Hong Kong

China's Soil Pollution and Degradation Problems

Claudio O. Delang

First published 2017
by Routledge
2 Park Square, Milton Park, Abingdon, Oxon OX14 4RN

and by Routledge
711 Third Avenue, New York, NY 10017

Routledge is an imprint of the Taylor & Francis Group, an informa business

British Library Cataloguing-in-Publication Data
A catalogue record for this book is available from the British Library

Library of Congress Cataloging-in-Publication Data
A catalog record for this book has been requested

ISBN: 978-1-138-68460-7 (hbk)
ISBN: 978-1-315-54371-0 (ebk)

Typeset in Times New Roman
by Apex CoVantage, LLC

Contents

Contents

1 Introduction

China's air pollution is infamous. The haze from belching factories and clogged highways can make it impossible to see buildings across the street. The pollution forces schools to close and creates health and morbidity problems, in addition to tremendous environmental degradation (Delang, 2016a). China's water pollution is less well known, especially for city dwellers who don't see the polluted rivers. However, news outlets frequently report on China's rivers mysteriously turning red or yellow, the sudden appearance of floating bodies of dead fish, and green algae blooms coloring lakes (Delang, 2016b).

China also faces another important environmental problem, which is less well known to the public: that of soil degradation and pollution. The problem of soil degradation is not unknown to Chinese people. In northern China, people have long been suffering from dust storms from the arid Loess Plateau, a problem which the government started to address in the 1980s through a series of environmental conservation programs. In the late 1990s the government also initiated the largest forest conservation and reforestation programs in the world, in most of the central and western provinces.

However, the problem and the extent of soil pollution are less known. People do know that not all the food they eat is healthy, but they do not know the scale of the problem. Indeed, up until very recently, little was known of the true extent of soil pollution in China, since the government has consistently refused to make comprehensive soil pollution data public. In 2013, Beijing's lawyer, Dong Zhengwei, requested soil pollution data from the Ministry of Environmental Protection, including information on the causes and methods for dealing with the problem. The request was declined on the grounds that the data was a "state secret". Nevertheless, at the end of 2013, the government released limited information on soil pollution, partly because of the strong public reaction against that refusal. Despite the lack of details, the released data caused widespread concern (He, 2014a). In April 2014, the government issued a more comprehensive report about the country's soils (He, 2014b). The report shows that 16.1 per cent of the soil samples (19.4 per cent for agricultural soils) are contaminated with organic and chemical contaminants as well as heavy metals and metalloids such as lead, cadmium, and arsenic (Zhao et al., 2014). Chinese officials say that an area the size of Taiwan is so polluted that farming should not be allowed there at all (Wong, 2014).

This book looks at the problems of soil degradation and pollution in China through a review of official reports, academic publications, and news articles published over the last years. After this short introduction, Chapter 2 discusses the levels of soil degradation and pollution. The chapter provides data about the soil resources in China in terms of agricultural land, grassland and forestland. It then turns to the national standards that are used to assess and quantify the level of pollution of soils and the geographic distribution of soil pollution. The third part of the chapter introduces the standards of soil erosion and the geographic distribution of degraded soils.

Chapter 3 looks at the causes of soil degradation and pollution. It first discusses the levels and the causes of soil degradation, touching on wind erosion, water erosion, and freeze-thaw erosion. The land-use practices that lead to soil erosion are mainly related to agricultural and livelihood activities and include overgrazing and the collection of fuelwood and medicinal plants. The chapter then reviews the different types of soil pollutants and their distribution in China. Soil pollution is caused by both agricultural and industrial activities. Pollution from agricultural activities includes the use of industrial wastewater and urban sewage, which farmers rely on to irrigate the soil because they lack sufficient water. In addition, soil is polluted by animal waste and the excessive use of fertilizers and pesticides. Pollution by industrial activities includes the accumulation of air pollutants in the soil resulting from mining, industrial activities, and transportation.

Chapter 4 discusses the impacts of soil degradation and soil pollution. Soil degradation results in nutrient loss, salinization, acidification, and desertification, with negative consequences on grain output and the production of livestock. Soil degradation also has negative consequences on ecosystem services, including damages to biodiversity, dust storms, and floods and landslides. The impact of soil pollution mainly affects China's food security and includes heavy metal contamination and food poisoning.

The government has started to address the problem of soil degradation from the 1980s with programs that aimed to restore the original vegetation on degraded lands. On the other hand, soil pollution has only started to be addressed over the last few years, partly because the problem is directly related to industrial activities, which the government does not want to curtail. As Zhuang Guotai, the head of the Ministry of Environmental Protection's Department of Nature and Ecology Conservation, said: "In comparison with efforts to clean up air and water pollution, we've hardly got started with soil. But once the market is opened up, soil remediation will be on a far bigger scale than either air or water cleanup" (He, 2014c).

Chapter 5 looks at the solutions to soil degradation and pollution. The approaches followed by the government to address soil degradation include the refinement of the legal framework, various land restoration policies (including the reforestation of dryland areas, a logging ban [the Natural Forest Protection Program], and the reforestation of wasteland and slope farmland [the Grain for Green Program]), and conservation agriculture. The solutions to soil pollution include improving the legal framework to punish polluters, identifying and monitoring the sources of pollution, and controlling the number of polluting enterprises. In addition, the government has proposed a reclassification of soil utilization to avoid employing polluted soil for agriculture, and promoting technologies to reduce soil pollutants. Not all policies pursued have been successful. For example, the reforestation of drylands has been blamed for contributing to desertification. However, it must be recognized that the government is finally acknowledging that soil degradation and pollution are problems which may imperil food security and jeopardize the development of the country and is trying to address the problem.

Bibliography

Delang, C. O. (2016a). *China's Air Pollution Problems*. London: Routledge.
Delang, C. O. (2016b). *China's Water Pollution Problems*. London: Routledge.
He, G. (2014a). Special report: The legacy of Hunan's polluted soils. *China Dialogue*. Retrieved 15 December 2016 from www.chinadialogue.net/article/show/single/en/7076-Special-report-the-legacy-of-Hunan-s-polluted-soils
He, G. (2014b). Special report: The victims of China's soil pollution crisis. *China Dialogue*. Retrieved 15 December 2016 from www.chinadialogue.net/article/show/single/en/7073-Special-report-The-victims-of-China-s-soil-pollution-crisis
He, G. (2014c). The soil pollution crisis in China: A cleanup presents daunting challenge. *Environment 360*. Retrieved 15 December 2016 from http://e360.yale.edu/feature/the_soil_pollution_crisis_in_china_a_cleanup_presents_daunting_challenge/2786/
Wong, E. (2014). One-fifth of China's farmland is polluted, state study finds. *The New York Times*. Retrieved 15 December 2016 from www.nytimes.com/2014/04/18/world/asia/one-fifth-of-chinas-farmland-is-polluted-state-report-finds.html
Zhao, F. J., Ma, Y., Zhu, Y. G., Tang, Z., & McGrath, S. P. (2014). Soil contamination in China: Current status and mitigation strategies. *Environmental Science & Technology, 49*(2), 750–759.

2 The levels of soil degradation and soil pollution

Introduction

Soils play a vital role in the Earth's ecosystem and are essential to human life. Soils filter the rainwater and regulate its discharge, preventing flooding. They also buffer against pollutants, protecting groundwater quality. Soils provide plants with a foothold for their roots and hold the necessary nutrients for plants to grow. They are home to a myriad of microorganisms that decompose organic matter, fix nitrogen, and store large amounts of organic carbon, all of which are fundamental processes for natural ecosystems. With 10 cm of topsoil taking more than 2,000 years to form, one could argue they are a non-renewable resource (Kong, 2015). Soils that have lost their fertility can be restored, but only at great pains and expense; therefore, prudent strategies for soil resource management are crucial for life on the planet (Rojas, 2013). In this chapter, I discuss the current conditions of soil resources in China. I will also provide an overview of Chinese soil quality standards and the classification, degree, and distribution of soil pollution and soil degradation in China. This will provide the background to the other chapters, where the causes, consequences, and solutions to soil pollution and degradation are presented.

Soil resources in China

Agricultural land

The past 50 years have brought a significant increase in China's agricultural productivity. The country's land area covers 6.4 percent of the world's total land area and 7.2 percent of its total farmland, and yet it supplies food to 22 per cent of the global population (Fan et al., 2011). According to China's Environmental State Bulletin released by the Ministry of Environmental Protection (MEP) in 2016, until the end of 2014, China had 645.7 million hectares of farmland, with arable land covering 135 million hectares, orchard land covering 14.4 million hectares, forestland (forestland is included in the official statistic of farmland) covering 253 million hectares, and pastureland covering 219.47 million hectares (MEP, 2016). However, the quality and quantity of land suitable for farming is dropping. The same study found that by the end of 2009, the country's land area suitable for cropping had shrunk to 0.1 ha per person over the previous three years, less than half the global average of 0.23 ha per person (China daily, 2014). In 2014, the amount of farmland had further dropped by 0.11 million hectares due to construction and natural disasters, among other reasons (MEP, 2016).

According to Liu et al. (2015), in the east of China, the area of farmland decreased mainly due to urban expansion and mining activities. On the other hand, in central and western China, the area of farmland decreased because of the Grain for Green conservation program, which involved converting croplands to woodlands and grasslands in areas with highly vulnerable ecosystems (Delang and Yuan, 2015). Finally, in the semi-arid and arid regions of northern China, the area of cropland increased due to the reclamation of grassland (Liu et al., 2015).

Apart from such regional changes, Xiao et al. (2015) also found that the ratio between irrigated farmland and rainfed farmland areas has changed significantly. Irrigated farmlands refer to agricultural lands where water is supplied to crops artificially, while rainfed farmlands receive their water from rainfall (Salmon et al., 2015). Irrigated farmland is usually more productive than rainfed farmland, because the timing – and amount – of water supplied to the plants can be regulated (most crops produce a larger harvest if they have plenty of water during the growing season).

As depicted in Figure 2.1, the area of irrigated farmlands dropped by 21 per cent between 1980 and 1990, and by a further 24 per cent between 2000 and 2010. Rainfed farmland areas followed the opposite trend, increasing from 1980 to 2010 (Xiao et al., 2015). According to Xiao et al. (2015), the reasons behind these changes are complex, but the most important reason for the decrease in irrigated farmland is related to the dramatic increase of urban population in the eastern provinces, which results in building factories and houses on irrigated farmland. On the other hand, the increase in rainfed farming is a result of land reclamation to satisfy the country's growing demand for food.

This increase in the proportion of rainfed farmlands adversely affected both the quality of arable land and the crop yield, because most rainfed land is cleared in areas that experience very unstable, unpredictable, and inconsistent precipitation, with dry spells and droughts that threaten agricultural output (FAO). Under such conditions, there is little prospect of increasing

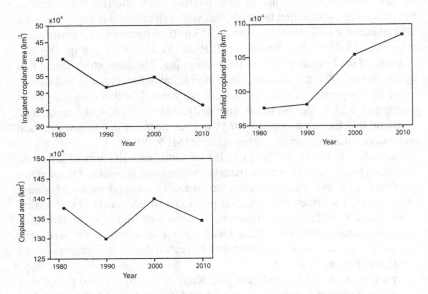

Figure 2.1 Total areas of irrigated and rainfed farmlands (1980–2010)
Note: 1 km² = 100 ha.
Source: Xiao et al. (2015)

crop yields. Cao et al. (2014) looked at the role irrigation plays in food production and concluded that the wheat yield of irrigated cropland was 170 per cent that of rainfed areas.

Grassland

In China, grasslands occur naturally in the dry areas in the north, in particular in Inner Mongolia and the elevated areas of the Tibetan Plateau. In many areas, in particular in the dryer Inner Mongolia, grassland is a vulnerable ecosystem that is sensitive to climatic variability and the effects of global warming, such as rising temperatures and less precipitation. Grasslands are also sensitive to human activities. In particular, excessive herding on pastureland has caused much environmental degradation in Inner Mongolia. As shown in Figure 2.2, China experienced a decline in grassland areas between 1980 and 2000. After 2000, the amount of grassland increased slightly and settled at 246.6 million ha in 2010, thanks to the program of "restoring cropland to grassland" that was launched nationwide (Xiao et al., 2015).

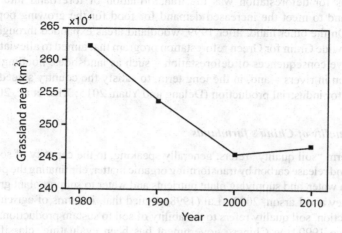

Figure 2.2 Total grassland area (1980–2010)

Source: Xiao et al. (2015)

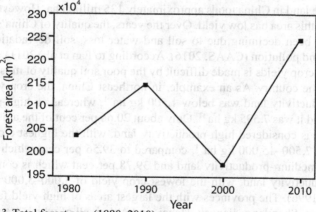

Figure 2.3 Total forest area (1980–2010)

Source: Xiao et al. (2015)

Forestland

The forest area of China expanded between 1981 and 1990, followed by a drop between 1990 and 2000, and expanded again until 2010 (Figure 2.3). The reasons behind this trend were manifold. However, one of the main reasons for deforestation was the transformation of forestland into new farmland to meet the increased demand for food for the growing population. On the other hand, after 1999, woodland areas expanded through the nationwide Grain for Green reforestation program that aimed to alleviate the negative consequences of deforestation – such as landslides, flooding, and siltation in rivers – and, in the long term, to satisfy the country's needs for wood for industrial production (Delang and Yuan, 2015; Xiao et al., 2015).

The quality of China's farmlands

The term "soil quality" refers, generally speaking, to the capacity of soils to hold and release carbon by transforming organic matter, eliminating the pollutants in water, and supplying plant nutrients and water to support plant growth (Keeney and Larson, 2000). Lal (1998) argued that, in terms of agricultural production, soil quality refers to the ability of soil to sustain production.

Since 1999, the Chinese government has been evaluating, classifying, and grading agricultural land for its quality, considering climatic factors, geographic factors, soil physical factors, and economic factors. This was the first systematic and comprehensive assessment of the condition of Chinese farmlands (Yang et al., 2014).

Arable land in China totals approximately 135 million ha. However, two-thirds of this area has low yield. Over the years, the quality of China's arable land has been declining due to soil and water loss, soil degradation processes, and pollution (CAAS, 2016). According to Fan et al. (2011), obtaining high crop yields is made difficult by the poor soil quality of most arable land in the country. As an example, in northeast China, the crop yield on low-productivity land was below 1,500 kg ha^{-1}, whereas on high-productivity land it was 7,595 kg ha^{-1}. Only about 20.66 per cent of the arable land in China is considered high-productivity land, with the highest crop yield between 7,500–15,000 kg ha^{-1}, compared to 39.56 per cent which is considered medium-productivity land and 39.78 per cent which is considered low-productivity land, with the lowest crop yield of 3,000–5,000 kg ha^{-1} (IOSC, 1996). The provinces with the largest areas of high-yield farmland are Henan, Shandong, Jiangsu, Hebei, and Anhui, all of which are situated on the Huang-Huai-Hai Plain (Ji et al., 2015).

Unfortunately, according to Kong (2014), there is no more spare land in China. The country has run out of available high-quality agricultural land that could be used to grow crops, as lands currently used for farming are being lost to development. At this point, converting forests and grasslands would only produce poor quality cropland, while also taking a serious ecological toll. Recent land-use figures indicate that the country is gradually exhausting what is left of its high-quality agricultural land (Kong, 2014). Fan et al. (2011) argued that despite its success in increasing agricultural production and crop yields, the annual growth rates of cereal yields in China are gradually decreasing. For example, the mean annual growth rates of grain yields dropped from 4 per cent in the 1970s to 1.9 per cent in the 1990s, and in most Chinese provinces, rice and maize yields have declined, or at best stagnated, over the last decade.

Soil pollution

China's soil problems are complicated, as there are many reasons for the low quality of farmland in the country. In this section, I first describe the standards developed to classify the levels and types of polluted soils and then discuss their geographic distribution.

Soil pollution standards

Soil contamination is a major contributor to poor soil health. Pollution of soils differs from water or air pollution in that it is usually not visible and can easily go undetected. It may take years from the beginning of pollution exposure to the discovery of harmful effects. Moreover, soil pollution may accumulate over time, and it is more difficult for the pollutants to migrate, diffuse, and dilute (Zhang, 2014).

Heavy metals in the soil are toxic for all living things, from microorganisms to plants and animals, and their removal from the soil is a cumbersome process. These toxins disturb and alter both natural and man-made ecosystems and may cause terminal diseases when transported to humans via the food web (Wang et al., 2001). Cadmium (Cd), for example, was recently detected in almost 50 per cent of the rice sampled in Guangzhou, the capital city of Guangdong Province. Prolonged exposure to this heavy metal can cause renal disease and tumors. Table 2.1 lists the most common pollutants found in Chinese soils, common items that may contain these chemical substances, some of their sources, and the conditions associated with exposure to them. Almost all of these contaminants are the by-products of industrial activities, mining operations, or coal burning or are emitted into the air with the exhaust fumes of vehicles (Hornby, 2015). However, pollutants are not limited to heavy metals. The waste material produced by livestock can also pollute the soil when it is washed into the soil with the water used for irrigation (Delang, 2016; Hsu and Miao, 2014). Excessive amounts of fertilizers and pesticides are also major sources of soil pollution.

In 1995, the Ministry of Environmental Protection (MEP) of China introduced the Environmental Quality Standard for Soils guidelines (GB 15618–1995) to inform citizens on the acceptable concentrations of soil contaminants and contamination measurement techniques (Zhang et al., 2015). The standard values, put into effect on 1 March

Table 2.1 Uses, sources, and potential damages of heavy metals

Heavy metals	Used in	Produced by	Condition
Cadmium (Cd)	Pigments and batteries	Coal and zinc mining and phosphate fertilizers	Painful joint swelling and bone deformities
Nickel (Ni)	Stainless steel and alloys	Burning oil and coal	Rashes and lung damage
Arsenic (As)	Gold mining, wood treatment, animal feed, and poisons	Mining waste	Withers crops and causes cancer
Copper (Cu)	Wiring, pipes, and alloys	Dust from mining and smelting and leaches from agricultural use	Diarrhea and nausea
Mercury (Hg)	Fluorescent bulbs, chemicals, coal burning, and gold production	Coal combustion and mining waste	Fatigue, physical deformities, and mental illnesses
Lead (Pb)	Batteries, paint, and solder	Coal burning, coal and metals mining, and smelting	Learning disabilities and stomach pains
Chromium (Cr)	Stainless steel and alloys	Waste from tanning	Hexavalent chromium is toxic
Zinc (Zn)	Galvanized steel and alloys	Mining and smelting waste and coal burning	Anemia and damage to the pancreas and kidneys

Source: Hornby (2015)

1996, were divided into three classes used for different soil functions (Table 2.2) (MEP, 1995).

- Class 1 values represent the natural background. This standard is used for nature reserves (except for the places with high soil environmental background value, meaning soils with naturally high proportions of heavy metals), centralized potable water sources, and some other soils requiring protection.
- Class 2 lands may be devoted to agriculture, since their level of pollution is considered safe for the production of food. For Class 2 soils, a distinction is made depending on the acidity or alkalinity of the soils, splitting the soils into three categories: soils with a pH value ≤ 6.5, soils with a pH value between 6.5 and 7.5, and soils with a pH value > 7.5, because different pH environments will influence the effects of the pollutants. These lands may be used as croplands or pasturelands. If the heavy metal concentrations of a soil exceed the maximum values

Table 2.2 Official Soil Environmental Standards in China (GB15618–1995) (mg/kg)

Chemical elements and pollutants		Class 1 (natural background)	Class 2			Class 3
			pH < 6.5	pH 6.5~7.5	pH > 7.5	pH > 6.5
Cadmium (Cd)	≤	0.2	0.3	0.3	0.6	1.0
Arsenic (As)	Paddy field ≤	15	30	25	20	30
	Dryland ≤	15	40	30	25	40
Mercury (Hg)	≤	0.15	0.3	0.5	1.0	1.5
Copper (Cu)	Cropland ≤	35	50	100	100	400
	Orchard ≤	–	150	200	200	400
Lead (Pb)	≤	35	250	300	350	500
Chromium (Cr)	Paddy field ≤	90	250	300	350	400
	Dryland ≤	90	150	200	250	300
Zinc (Zn)	≤	100	200	250	300	500
Nickel (Ni)	≤	40	40	50	60	200
Dichlorodiphenyl-Trichloroethane (DDT)	≤	0.05		0.50		1.0
Hexachlorocycl-Ohexane (C6H6Cl6)	≤	0.05		0.50		1.0

Source: MEP (1995)

defined in Class 2, it is rated as too contaminated for growing grains for consumption.
• Class 3 land cannot be used for farming. Lands with such high levels of heavy metal contamination may be found near factories and mines, but in some cases such high levels of heavy metals may also be natural (MEP, 1995). If the concentrations are higher than the values in Class 3, the plants will stop growing and probably die.

Geographic distribution of soil pollution

In April 2014, the Ministry of Environmental Protection (MEP) and the Ministry of Land and Resources (MLR) of China published a collaborative evaluation of the conditions of the country's soils. This was the first time that the government carried out an assessment of the country's soil pollution and released it to the public (MEP, 2014). The evaluation built on in-depth analyses of soils carried out between 2005 and 2013, sampling soils from over 70 per cent of the country's land area. Of all the samples analyzed, 16.1 per cent of the soil examined was found to be contaminated with heavy metals such as Cd, As, Pb, and Hg. Unsurprisingly, since the excessive use of fertilizers contributes to pollution, the highest proportion of areas exceeding the national quality standards came from farmlands: 19.4 per cent of the land used for agricultural activities was contaminated with heavy metals (Table 2.3). Assuming that the polluted areas are proportional to the number of surveyed samples, this means that about 26 million ha were contaminated. The vice minister, Wang Shiyuan, acknowledged that an additional area of 3.31 million hectares of agricultural land was contaminated to a smaller degree (He, 2014a). In addition, another 3.2 million hectares were found to be so contaminated that agricultural practices should be banned there (Wong, 2014). Unfortunately, although this soil quality report represented an important step toward the country's openness regarding pollution, it failed to shed light on crucial details and did not offer solutions to China's pollution problems (Bale, 2014).

Soil pollution in China tends to be localized. Soil pollution is more severe in the south than the north, particularly in the Yangtze River Delta, Pearl River Delta, and the traditional industrial base in south-east China. Heavy metal pollution is prevalent in the southern, central, and southwestern regions (Xinhua, 2014) (Figure 2.4), with the main pollutants being Cd, Ni, Hg, and As. As stated by Zhao et al. (2014), lands in some regions, especially those close to mines and industries, have been suffering from severe pollution, and the quality of soils dedicated to growing crops should also be given particular attention. Compared to a previous small-scale survey conducted during the 1980s (referred to in Zhang, 2014), available data indicate a significant

Table 2.3 Degrees of soil contamination according to ecosystem types

Ecosystem type	Per cent of land polluted	Degrees of exceedance in these area			
		Slight (1)	Light (2)	Moderate (3)	Severe (4)
Nationwide	16.1 per cent	11.2 per cent	2.3 per cent	1.5 per cent	1.1 per cent
Farmland	19.4 per cent	13.7 per cent	2.8 per cent	1.8 per cent	1.1 per cent
Woodland	10.0 per cent	5.9 per cent	1.6 per cent	1.2 per cent	1.3 per cent
Grassland	10.4 per cent	7.6 per cent	1.2 per cent	0.9 per cent	0.7 per cent
Unused	11.4 per cent	8.4 per cent	1.1 per cent	0.9 per cent	1.0 per cent

Notes: The degree of soil pollution in this table is divided into four levels, based on the Type 2 quality standards of Table 2.2.: Slight (1) exceeds Type 2 quality standards less than 2 times; Light (2) exceeds Type 2 quality standards between 2 and 3 times; Moderate (3) exceeds Type 2 quality standards between 3 and 5 times; Severe (4) exceeds Type 2 quality standards over 5 times. Soil that does not exceed Type 2 quality standards is not polluted (MEP, 2014).

Source: The national soil pollution condition investigation communique (MEP, 2014)

increase in inorganic pollutants in surface soils. On the other hand, the increase in Cd content has affected soils all over the country, with a 50 per cent rise in the coastal and southwestern regions and a 10 per cent to 40 per cent rise in the eastern, northeastern, and western areas of China (Zhang, 2014).

A number of scholars, apart from the MEP, have attempted to estimate the degree and distribution of soil contamination in China. One of the most comprehensive studies was carried out by Yang et al. (2014), who used the standards of Table 2.2 but included only As, Cr, Cd, Hg, and Pb because they are the most common. Based on the standards presented in Table 2.2, Yang et al. (2014) defined new soil classes (reproduced in Table 2.4). Yang et al. (2014) adopted the veto method to assess the level of pollution in each soil sample: the environmental quality class of each soil sample is determined by the lowest environmental quality class of its individual chemical elements. For example, if the environmental quality classifications for As, Cr, Cd, Hg, and Pb of one soil sample are classes 4, 2, 3, 2, and 2, respectively, then the environmental quality class of that soil sample is 4.

Yang et al. (2014) provide a detailed assessment of the environmental quality classes of China's soils (Figure 2.4). While they found low levels of soil pollution, their sampling was biased: "The sampling sites were selected avoiding polluted areas, including a major road, a railway, and obviously contaminated areas. In terms of timing, samples were collected at the time without fertilizing" (Yang et al., 2014: 128). Using such approach, they found that areas with clean soil and relatively clean soil account for 60.3 per cent and 29.5 per cent of the study area, respectively, whereas areas with polluted and moderately polluted soils account for only 1.8 per cent and

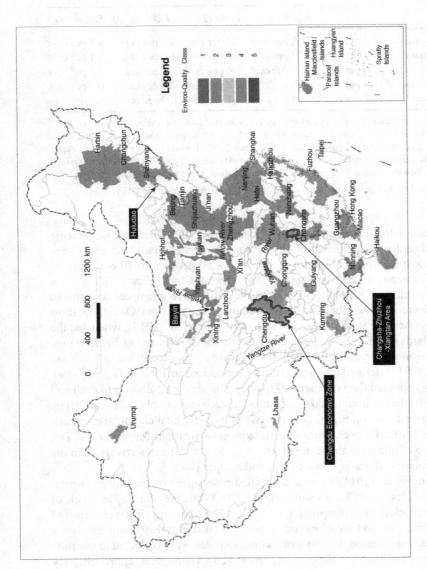

Figure 2.4 Distribution of polluted soil

Note: See Table 2.4 for the data for Classes 1–5 in the figure.

Source: Yang et al. (2014)

Table 2.4 Classification and definitions of soil pollution levels used by Yang et al. (2014), based on Table 2.2

Class	Level of pollution
1. Clean	Less than the standard for type 1
2. Relatively clean	Between the standards for types 1 and 2
3. Normal	Between the standards for types 2 and 3
4. Polluted	Greater than the standard for type 3 and less than twice the standard for type 3
5. Moderately to heavily polluted	Greater than twice the standard for type 3

Source: Yang et al. (2014)

0.8 per cent, respectively. Presumably, this leaves 7.6 per cent of "normal" soil with a level of pollution between the standards for types 2 and 3 (Table 2.4).

According to Yang et al. (2014), there are different reasons for the anomalous enrichment of harmful chemicals in the soil in different areas. In densely populated cities and developed mining areas, such as the Changsha – Zhuzhou – Xiangtan area in Hunan Province, Shenyang and Huludao in Liaoning Province, and Baiyin in Gansu Province, high contents of harmful chemicals such as As and Cd in the soil are primarily caused by human activities. However, most of these areas are urban, industrial, or mining lands rather than agricultural lands. In essence, they found that in most cases, pollution does not have a significant effect on food security, although the exclusion of visibly polluted areas has biased the findings and makes these conclusions somewhat questionable (Yang et al., 2014).

Other researchers obtained contrasting results to those found by Yang et al. (2014). As an example, Zhang et al. (2015) looked at the pollution rates of farmland soils and found that the soil in Tianjin Municipality was highly polluted, with a pollution rate of 70 per cent, resulting from the use of sewage water for the irrigation of arable land. In addition, they found that 55.93 per cent of the agricultural lands of Guizhou Province, 36.25 per cent of those in Hunan Province, 38.75 per cent of those in Guangdong Province, and 30.80 per cent of those in the Guangxi Zhuang Autonomous Region were polluted, due to the intense mining and smelting processes and the large number of chemical manufacturing plants in these provinces (Figure 2.5).

Another region suffering from soil pollution is Hunan Province, a major heavy metal production hub of China. The province is home to 1,003 nonferrous metal enterprises that, in 2011, were responsible for China's third largest production output of 2.66 million tons of ten different metals, a business worth $60 billion (He, 2014b). The government has been trying to control the pollution in Hunan Province for many years. However, in January 2016, an

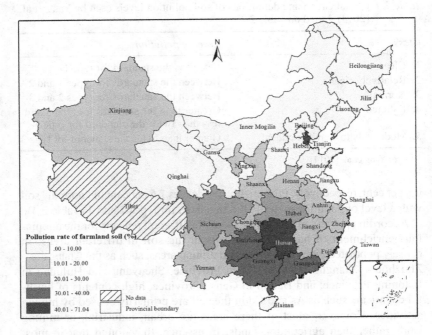

Figure 2.5 Pollution rate of farmland soil by heavy metals at the provincial level

Source: Zhang et al. (2015)

official of the Non-Ferrous Metals Management Bureau of Hunan Province acknowledged that the Xiang River basin (in Hunan Province) had almost 1,000 tailings and sludge disposal sites, accommodating 440 million tons of solid waste polluted with Pb, Hg, and Cd (He, 2014b). Chen Chao's statement made it clear that Hunan Province was responsible for 32.1 per cent of China's Cd emissions, 20.6 per cent of its As emissions, 58.7 per cent of its Hg emissions, and 24.6 per cent of its Pb emissions. According to official data, 13 per cent of the total area of Hunan Province, about 11,000 square miles, has been contaminated with waste and heavy metals from mines (He, 2014b).

Hunan is also an important producer of rice, growing approximately 30 million tons annually, which is about 15 per cent of the total rice output of the country. Unfortunately, the polluted land ends up producing polluted grains. A study on the rice grain quality of a county situated in the Xiangjiang River basin in Hunan province revealed that 60 per cent of the rice samples exceeded the 0.2 mg Cd kg^{-1} limit (adopted by China), and 11 per cent contained > 1.0 mg Cd kg^{-1} (Zhao et al., 2014). Market basket studies examining the country-level contamination of rice grain concluded that between 2 per cent and 13 per cent of the samples exceeded the limit. According to Zhao et al.,

> Cd intake from rice alone with a Cd concentration of 0.2 mg kg^{-1} would amount to 0.73 and 1.01 µg kg^{-1} body weight day^{-1} for the national average (for adults of 65 kg body weight); the latter already exceeds the FAO/WHO tolerable daily intake (TDI) of 0.83 µg kg^{-1} body weight day^{-1}.
>
> (Zhao et al., 2014: 753)

Researchers determined that the dietary exposure to Cd for people living in close proximity to mines significantly exceeded the tolerable daily intake level, and rice was identified as the primary source. Moreover, a connection between prolonged exposure to Cd and kidney disease, osteoporosis, and increased cancer mortality rates has also been found among people living in close proximity to mines. Besides Cd, the high levels of toxic Pb and As found in rice are also a cause for concern. An analysis of rice grown near the mining sites in Hunan Province determined that 65, 50, and 34 per cent of the samples exceeded the Chinese limits for Cd, As, and Pb concentration in food, respectively (Zhao et al., 2014).

Soil degradation

The standards for soil degradation

Over the last decades, with the rapid economic development and population growth, soil degradation, including soil erosion, land desertification, soil salinization, soil impoverishment, and soil pollution, has become an increasingly serious problem (He, 2014b; Zhang, 2014). However, determining the severity of pollution and combating soil erosion in China is a major undertaking. The complicated environmental conditions and lack of fieldwork and onsite examination make it challenging to precisely measure the properties of soil and the degree of erosion throughout the country (Wang et al., 2016). Furthermore, as Wang et al. (2016) emphasize, it is challenging to establish comprehensive standards to evaluate soil erosion, as the soils are affected by a combination of wind, water, and freeze-thaw erosion simultaneously.

As there are no comprehensive standards for soil erosion in China, the MEP (2003) has developed indicators of soil erosion based on the classification and gradation of soil erosion (SL190–2007) and other regional guidelines by China's Ministry of Water Resources. Based on these sources, soil erosion can be classified into five categories according to severity: slight, moderate, high, severe, and extreme (MEP, 2003). Table 2.5 shows the prevalence and characteristics of each category.

Table 2.5 Indicators of soil erosion degree

Degree	Area of soil erosion (per cent)	Vegetation coverage (per cent)	Decrease of land biological productivity (per cent)
Slight	< 10	> 70	< 10
Moderate	< 10	70~50	10~30
High	10~30	50~30	30~50
Severe	30~50	30~10	50~70
Extreme	> 50	< 10	> 70

Source: MEP (2003)

The amount of soil degradation

China is suffering from the most severe soil erosion and degradation in the world (Table 2.6). There are approximately 4.52 billion tons of eroded soil per year, accounting for approximately one-fifth of the total global soil erosion (Zhang, 2014). According to Daily News (2015), the country's arable land is disappearing at a speed of 400,000 hectares per year, with the surface soil in the northern Chinese Loess Plateau losing one centimeter annually. The official news agency, Xinhua, reported that over 40 percent of the fertile land has been degraded, which raises the question whether China will be able to continue to satisfy its own demand for food (Patton, 2014).

China also shows an alarming tendency to convert increasing areas of cultivated land for urban development. Between the 1960s and 1980s, 538,000 ha per year were converted. Between 1986 and 1995, a further 680,000 ha of cultivated land was converted, an area that would have been able to produce 3 million tons of grains. These changes have increased the pressure on the remaining cultivated land (Berry, 2003). To slow down the conversion of farmland into other uses, the Chinese government introduced the Basic Farmland Protection Regulation in 1994. This law was meant to prevent the conversion of high-quality, highly productive farmland to non-agricultural uses, without specific government approval. In 1999, the government introduced the Land Administration Law to expand the measure to lower-quality agricultural land (Liu et al., 2014). It is questionable how effective these laws have been, since the amount of irrigated cropland has dropped considerably from 2000 to 2010 (see Figure 2.1).

According to a countrywide survey conducted in 2008, if soil erosion continues at its present rate, almost 100 million people in southwest China could lose the land they live on within 35 years (Branigan, 2008). As the

Table 2.6 Severity of soil erosion in China based on total land area and soil erosion amount (SEM) (1 Mg = 1 megagram, or 1 metric ton)

Soil erosion intensity (SEI)	Area		Soil erosion amount (SEM)	
	Millions of ha	*%*	*Millions of Mg*	*%*
Slight	105.13	60.75	1,013.88	11.43
Moderate	31.46	18.18	859.92	9.69
High	12.67	7.32	704.53	7.94
Severe	10.68	6.17	1,084.27	12.22
Extreme	13.11	7.58	3,839.00	43.26

Source: Rao et al. (2015)

topsoil is blown away by wind and washed away by rain across one-third of the country, the sources of grains and water suffer irreversible damage (UN News Centre, 2010).

The distribution of soil erosion in China

Rao et al. (2015) looked at the soil erosion rates in different habitats and found that the areas of greatest concern are croplands, followed by grasslands and shrublands. Forests had the lowest soil erosion rates, after bare lands and deserts (Table 2.7). This is not surprising, since precipitation and wind are two of the most important factors that cause soil erosion in natural habitats. According to Figure 2.5, 32.72 per cent of the eroded areas in China are croplands, even though they make up only 19.14 per cent of the total area of China. The numbers are even worse when one only looks at the amount of soil that is eroded. Over half of all the soil eroded in China comes from croplands (56.29 per cent of the total) even though they only make up 19.14 per cent of the total land area (Table 2.7). This is obviously very worrisome, considering that, as mentioned earlier, there is no other land that can be used for farming once the currently cultivated lands lose their fertility.

High soil erosion rates on farmland are partly due to farming practices – the fact that the topsoil is frequently disturbed when hoed and that the surface is bare during part of the year and therefore easily eroded by wind and rain – and partly to the poor choice of the land, in particular the cultivation on steep slopes. The soil erosion of steep slope lands has been addressed by the Grain for Green project, which withdraws from cultivation the lands have the highest risk of erosion (see Chapter 5). However, while this program reduces soil erosion, it also reduces the total amount of farmland under cultivation, so does not address the growing problem of a dwindling food supply.

Table 2.7 Soil erosion in different ecosystems in China by total land area, soil erosion area, soil erosion amount, and soil erosion rate from 2000 to 2010. (1 Mg = 1 megagram, or 1 metric ton)

Ecosystem types	Area		Soil erosion area (SEA)		Soil erosion amount (SEM)		Soil erosion rate (SER)
	Millions of ha	%	Millions of ha	%	Millions of Mg	%	Mg ha^{-1} yr^{-1}
Forest	190.78	20.19	17.49	10.11	367.99	3.02	1.40
Shrub	69.92	7.40	36.71	21.21	864.33	9.74	12.36
Grassland	284.52	30.11	54.89	31.72	1,923.00	21.67	6.76
Cropland	180.91	19.14	56.62	32.72	4,995.17	56.29	27.61
City	25.43	2.69	0.87	0.50	71.88	0.81	2.83
Desert	44.94	4.76	0.75	0.43	33.72	0.38	0.76
Bare land	106.59	11.28	5.73	3.31	717.91	8.09	6.74

Source: Rao et al. (2015)

Rao et al. (2015) found that shrublands had the second highest soil erosion rates, almost half of that in croplands. This is due to the fact that shrubs are often the secondary vegetation that colonizes degraded forest areas after prolonged environmental stress. Natural shrublands are biomes that receive little precipitation, usually less than 250 mm annually, and therefore are sensitive to wind erosion and desertification. In recent years, due to global warming, precipitation has further decreased in these areas (Rao et al., 2015).

Shrublands were followed by grasslands and bare lands in terms of soil erosion rates (Table 2.7). Grassland areas experience erosion as a consequence of low precipitation, high grazing pressure, and difficulty in implementing soil conservation measures in many of the areas where grassland is the predominant land cover, in particular in Inner Mongolia (Briske et al., 2015; Wen et al., 2015). Finally, deserts had the lowest soil erosion rates, since the biome has already been heavily eroded and cannot worsen.

Geographic distribution of soil erosion

Severe soil erosion affects areas in the provinces of Shanxi, Gansu, Shaanxi, Ningxia, and Inner Mongolia, all located in the central region of the Yellow River, as well as Yunnan, Sichuan, Guizhou, and Chongqing Provinces, upstream of the Yangtze River (Figure 2.6) (Rao et al., 2015).

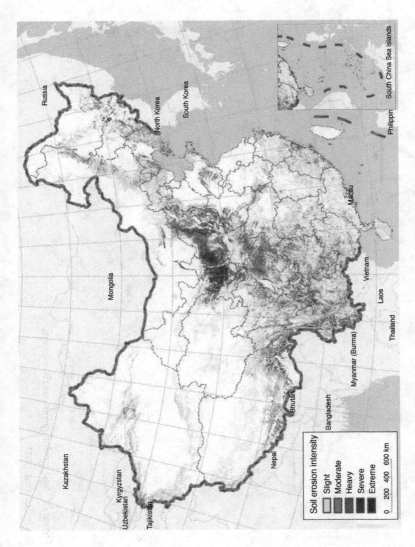

Figure 2.6 Geographical distribution and severity of soil erosion in China

Source: Rao et al. (2015)

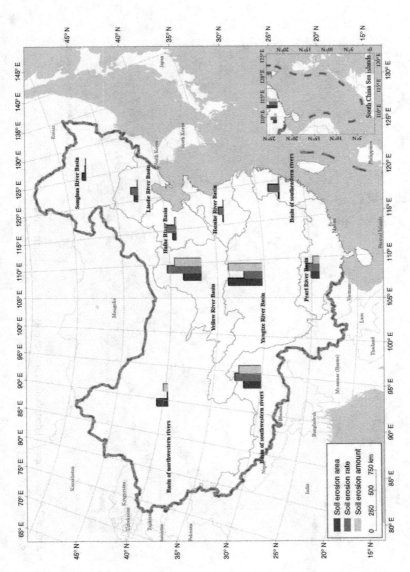

Figure 2.7 Soil erosion in various river basins

Source: Rao et al. (2015)

The largest areas affected by soil erosion are in the Yangtze River basin and the Yellow River basin, followed by the basins of the southwestern rivers (Figure 2.7). The amount of soil erosion in the Yangtze River basin is of an astonishing 2,706.19 million Mg (1 Mg = 1 metric ton), 2,169.72 million Mg in the Yellow River Basin and 1,814.72 million Mg in the basins of the southwestern rivers (Rao et al., 2015). Most of the eroded soil is the more productive topsoil.

The Yellow River is also called the "Mother River of China" or "the Cradle of Chinese Civilization", as its basin was the most prosperous region in ancient Chinese history and the origin of the northern Chinese civilizations. However, it is also one of the most heavily eroded areas of the country. A report released by the Yellow River Conservancy Commission has found that 62 per cent of the area of the Yellow River basin has been eroded. This is one of the most devastating manifestations of soil erosion in the world (WWF Global, 2015). According to the WWF report, a 46.5 million ha area of the Yellow River basin is affected by water and soil erosion. Although the effective control of soil and sand in the areas prone to erosion keeps 350 million to 450 million tons of silt from pouring into the river, saving almost 22.6 million ha of land from erosion every year, better practices to conserve and protect the Yellow River basin are still a dire necessity (WWF Global, 2015).

Guo et al. (2015) compared the rates of rainfall, soil loss, and runoff across different regions that are affected by erosion: the black soil region in the northeast (NE); the northern (N) rocky and earth mountain region; the Loess Plateau region in the northwest (NW); the purple soil region in southwest China (SW); and the hilly red soil region in southern China (S) (Figure 2.8). In general, the amount of rain and, thus, the amount of runoff in northern China (NE, N and NW) was smaller than in southern China (SW and S) (Figure 2.8C). As expected, there is a positive correlation between rainfall (Figure 2.8C) and runoff (Figure 2.8A). The lowest and highest amounts of rainfall and runoff were in the NW and S regions, respectively. On the other hand, soil loss rates were approximately the same in the NW and southern parts of China (SW and S) (Figure 2.8B). According to Guo et al. (2015), the high rates of soil loss with small amounts of runoff in the NW were likely due to the properties of the soil in the area, which is characterized by low organic matter levels, poorly formed soil structure, and a strong tendency toward erosion. As a result, the NW region experienced small water discharges with a huge sediment load.

Rao et al. (2015)'s study found that all 31 provinces and provincial-level administrative units in China were suffering from soil erosion, with the

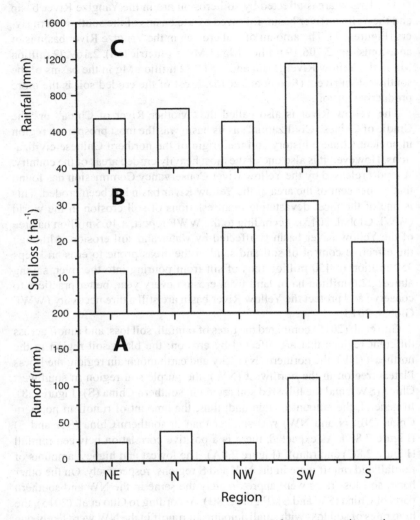

Figure 2.8 Rainfall, runoff, and soil loss rates across five water erosion regions
Source: Guo et al. (2015)

most severely affected areas being Sichuan, Yunnan, and Tibet Provinces
(Figure 2.9A). The provinces with the highest soil erosion rates included
Chongqing, Shanxi, and Shaanxi (Figure 2.9B). Most areas suffering from
the greatest amounts of eroded soil were located in western China, namely

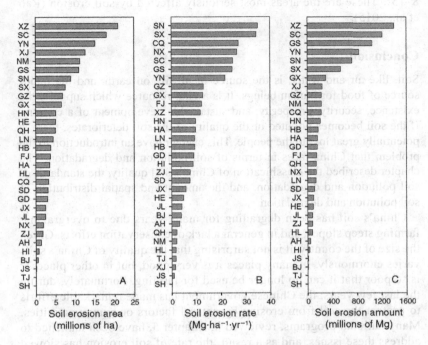

Figure 2.9 Soil erosion (1 Mg = 1 metric ton) in various provinces (autonomous regions/municipalities)

Note: AH, Anhui; BJ, Beijing; CQ, Chongqing; FJ, Fujian; GD, Guangdong; GS, Gansu; GX, Guangxi; GZ, Guizhou; HA, Henan; HB, Hubei; HE, Hebei; HI, Hainan; HL, Heilongjiang; HN, Hunan; JL, Jilin; JS, Jiangsu; JX, Jiangxi; LN, Liaoning; NM, Inner Mongolia; NX, Ningxia; QH, Qinghai; SC, Sichuan; SD, Shandong; SH, Shanghai; SN, Shaanxi; SX, Shanxi; TJ, Tianjin; XJ, Xinjiang; XZ, Tibet; YN, Yunnan; ZJ, Zhejiang.

Source: Rao et al. (2015)

Gansu, Sichuan, and Tibet, making up approximately 76.15 per cent of the total eroded land in the country (Figure 2.9C). Tibet experiences large soil erosion mainly because the Tibetan Plateau is easily eroded due to its high elevations at 3000–4000 m ASL, which prevents the growth of trees. On the other hand, Shaanxi, Shanxi, Gansu, Chongqing, and Sichuan Provinces include a large portion of the total area affected by soil erosion, mainly because the Yangtze River basin contains many areas with slopes of 15–25° and the Yellow River basin contains many areas with slopes of

8–15°. These are the areas most seriously affected by soil erosion (Rao et al., 2015).

Conclusion

Soil, like air and water, is the source of all life on earth, and the major source of food for human beings. It is a vital resource which supports the existence, security, prosperity, and sustainable development of a country. If the soil becomes polluted or the quality of the soil deteriorates, there is potentially great loss to the people. This chapter gave an introduction to the problem that China faces in terms of soil pollution and degradation. The chapter described the classification of China's soil quality, the standards of soil pollution and degradation, and the amount and spatial distribution of soil pollution and degradation.

China's soil has been degrading for many years due to overgrazing, farming steep slopes, and in general a lack of conservation efforts. Given the size of the country, it is not surprising that the quality of China's soils varies enormously. In many places it is very good, but in other places it is so poor that it can no longer be used for farming. Fortunately, during the last few years, the Chinese government has made remarkable efforts to protect the soil from erosion by natural factors or human activities. Many national programs, reviewed in Chapter 5, have been launched to address these issues, and as a result, the rate of soil erosion has slowed down.

On the other hand, soil pollution is more difficult to tackle because it is more difficult to monitor, and it is caused by the production of food (when the pollution is the result of the excessive application of fertilizers and pesticides) or by economic activities (when it results from mining and smelting processes, chemical manufacturing plants, or the exhaust of polluted fumes from manufacturing industries or vehicles). Addressing soil pollution is more expensive than addressing soil degradation because it is expensive to remove pollutants from the soil, and it involves reforming the economic activities that are the backbone of the Chinese economy. This can only be done at high economic costs, which in the present climate of a slowing economy is difficult to implement or justify. Nevertheless, China has finally officially acknowledged that there is a problem with its soils, and is starting to address it.

The next chapter will look at the causes of soil degradation and soil pollution in China. This will lay the groundwork for Chapter 4, which will look at the consequences, and Chapter 5, which will look at the efforts expended to try to improve the situation. China is faced with tremendous challenges when dealing with the soil pollution problems, including the absence of laws and regulations, the ambiguity of liability, the lack of accountability, and the poor management record (CCICED, 2015).

Bibliography

Bale, R. (October, 2014). China's other pollution problem – its soil. *Reveal*. Retrieved 15 December 2016 from www.revealnews.org/article-legacy/chinas-other-pollution-problem-its-soil/

Berry, L. (2003). Land Degradation in China: Its Extent and Impact. Commissioned by Global Mechanism with Support from the World Bank. Report submitted to the United Nations.

Branigan, T. (2008). Soil erosion threatens land of 100m Chinese, survey finds. *The Guardian*. Retrieved 15 December 2016 from www.theguardian.com/world/2008/nov/21/china-soil-erosion-population

Briske, D. D., Zhao, M., Han, G., Xiu, C., Kemp, D. R., Willms, W., Havstad, K., Kang, L., Wang, Z., Wu, J., Han, X., & Bai, Y. (2015). Strategies to alleviate poverty and grassland degradation in Inner Mongolia: Intensification vs production efficiency of livestock systems. *Journal of Environmental Management*, *152*, 177–182.

CAAS. (2016). Agriculture in China. China Academic of Agricultural Sciences. Retrieved from www.caas.cn/en/agriculture/agriculture_in_china/

Cao, X. C., Wu, P. T., Wang, Y. B., & Zhao, X. N. (2014). Assessing blue and green water utilization in wheat production of China from the perspectives of water footprint and total water use. *Hydrology and Earth System Sciences*, *18*(8), 3165–3178.

CCICED. (2015). Special Policy Study on Soil Pollution Management. China Council for International Cooperation on Environment and Development. Paper presented at the 3rd work meeting CCICED Special Policy Study on Soil Pollution Management, Shanghai, 21–23 July 2015. Retrieved 15 December 2016 from www.cciced.net/encciced/policyresearch/report/201511/P020151117574528584858.pdf

China daily. (November, 2014). More than 40 per cent of China's arable land degraded: Report. *China Daily*. Retrieved 15 December 2016 from www.chinadaily.com.cn/china/2014-11/05/content_18871081.htm

Daily News. (2015). China's soil erosion area accounts for 30 per cent of land loss per mu of cultivated land per year. (中国水土流失面积占国土3成 每年损失百万亩耕地) Retrieved 15 December 2016 from http://news.163.com/15/1103/01/B7F8TP9O00014AEE.html

Delang, C. O. (2016). *China's Water Pollution Problems*. London: Routledge.

Delang, C. O., & Yuan, Z. (2015). *China's Grain for Green Program*. Heidelberg: Springer.

Duggan, J. (April, 2014). One fifth of China's farmland polluted. *The Guardian*. Retrieved 15 December 2016 from www.theguardian.com/environment/chinas-choice/2014/apr/18/china-one-fifth-farmland-soil-pollution

Fan, M. S., Shen, J. B., Yuan, L. X., Jiang, R. F., Chen, X. P., Davies, W. J., & Zhang, F. (2011). Improving crop productivity and resource use efficiency to ensure food security and environmental quality in China. *Journal of Experimental Botany*, *63*(1), 13–24.

FAO. *The Use of Water in Agriculture*. Rome: FAO. Retrieved 15 December 2016 from www.fao.org/docrep/006/y4683e/y4683e07.htm

Gbtimes Beijing. (November, 2015). 30 per cent of Chinese land suffering soil erosion. *Global Times*. Retrieved 15 December 2016 from http://gbtimes.com/china/30-chinese-land-suffering-soil-erosion

Guo, Q. K., Hao, Y. F., & Liu, B. Y. (2015). Rates of soil erosion in China: A study based on runoff plot data. *Catena, 124*, 68–76. DOI: 10.1016/j.catena.2014.08.013

He, G. (July, 2014a). Special report: The legacy of Hunan's polluted soils. *China Dialogue*. Retrieved 15 December 2016 from www.chinadialogue.net/article/show/single/en/7076-Special-report-the-legacy-of-Hunan-s-polluted-soils

He, G. (July, 2014b). The soil pollution crisis in China: A cleanup presents daunting challenge. *Yale Environment 360*. Retrieved 15 December 2016 from http://e360.yale.edu/mobile/feature.msp?id=2786

Hornby, L. (September, 2015). Chinese environment: Ground operation. *Financial Times*. Retrieved 15 December 2016 from www.ft.com/content/d096f594-4be0-11e5-b558-8a9722977189

Hsu, A., & Miao, W. (June, 2014). Soil pollution in China still a state secret. *Scientific American*. Retrieved 15 December 2016 from http://blogs.scientificamerican.com/guest-blog/soil-pollution-in-china-still-a-state-secret-infographic/

IOSC. (October, 1996). *White Paper: The Grain Issue in China*. Beijing: Information Office of the State Council of the People's Republic of China. Retrieved 15 December 2016 from www.iatp.org/files/Grain_Issue_in_China_White_Paper_The.htm

Ji, Y. Z., Yan, H. M., Liu, J. Y., Kuang, W. H., & Hu, Y. F. (2015). A MODIS data derived spatial distribution of high-, medium- and low-yield cropland in China (in Chinese). *Acta Geographica Sinica, 70*(5).

Jin, B. (January, 2010). Sixty years of industrialization in China. Retrieved 15 December 2016 from http://english.qstheory.cn/economics/201109/t20110924_112480.htm

Keeney, D., & Larson, W. (2000). Departments-Viewpoint-Asia-Pacific: A case for improving soil quality. *Chemical Innovation, 30*(9), 48–51.

Kong, A. (May, 2015). No quick fix for China's polluted soil. *South China Morning Post*. Retrieved 15 December 2016 from www.scmp.com/comment/insight-opinion/article/1783358/no-quick-fix-chinas-polluted-soil

Kong, X. (February, 2014). China must protect high-quality arable land. *Nature, 506*, 7.

Lal, R. (1998). Soil quality and agricultural sustainability. In: Lal, R. (Ed.) *Soil Quality and Agricultural Sustainability*. London: CRC Press, Ch. 1, pp. 3–12.

Liu, L., Xu, X. L., Liu, J. Y., Chen, X., & Ning, J. (2015). Impact of farmland changes on production potential in China during 1990–2010. *Journal of Geographical Sciences, 25*(1), 19–34.

Liu, Y., Fang, F., & Li, Y. (2014). Key issues of land use in China and implications for policy making. *Land Use Policy, 40*, 6–12.

MEP. (1995). *Environmental Quality Standards for Soils* (in Chinese). Beijing: Ministry of Environmental Protection. Retrieved 15 December 2016 from http://kjs.mep.gov.cn/hjbhbz/bzwb/trhj/trhjzlbz/199603/W020070313485587994018.pdf

MEP. (2003). *Temporary Regulation of Ecological Function Zoning* (生态功能区划暂行规程) (in Chinese). Beijing: Ministry of Environmental Protection.

Retrieved 15 December 2016 from http://sts.mep.gov.cn/stbh/stglq/200308/ t20030815_90755.shtml

MEP. (2014). *The National Soil Pollution Condition Investigation Communique* (土地污染调查公报) (in Chinese). Beijing: Ministry of Environmental Protection. Retrieved 15 December 2016 from www.gov.cn/foot/site1/20140417/782b cb88840814ba158d01.pdf

MEP. (June, 2015). *National Land and Agricultural Environment in 2014* (2014 年土地与农村环境) (in Chinese). Beijing: Ministry of Environmental Protection Retrieved 15 December 2016 from www.mep.gov.cn/hjzl/trhj/201605/ t20160526_347133.shtml

MEP. (June, 2016). *National Land and Agricultural Environment in 2015* (2015 年土地与农村环境) (in Chinese). Beijing: Ministry of Environmental Protection Retrieved 15 December 2016 from www.mep.gov.cn/hjzl/trhj/201606/ t20160602_353282.shtml

Patton, D. (November, 2014). More than 40 percent of China's arable land degraded: Xinhua. Retrieved 15 December 2016 from www.reuters.com/article/us-china-soil-idUSKBN0IO0Y720141104

Rao, E., Xiao, Y., Ouyang, Z., & Yu, X. (2015). National assessment of soil erosion and its spatial patterns in China. *Ecosystem Health and Sustainability, 1*(4), 13. Retrieved from http://dx.doi.org/10.1890/EHS14-0011.1

Rojas, N. (2013). *An Overview of the Geospatial Methodologies Used in Order to Assess the Soil Erosion Risk by Water*. Madrid: Comisión Nacional de Actividades Espaciales (Conae). Retrieved 15 December 2016 from http://aulavirtual.ig.conae. gov.ar/moodle/pluginfile.php/513/mod_page/content/96/Soil%20Erosion_2013.pdf

Salmon, J. M., Friedl, M. A., Frolking, S., Wisser, D., & Douglas, E. M. (2015). Global rain-fed, irrigated, and paddy croplands: A new high resolution map derived from remote sensing, crop inventories and climate data. *International Journal of Applied Earth Observation and Geoinformation, 38*, 321–334. Retrieved from http://dx.doi.org/10.1016/j.jag.2015.01.014

UN News Centre. (December, 2010). Land degradation among China's food supply challenges, says UN expert. Retrieved 15 December 2016 from www.un.org/apps/ news/story.asp?NewsID=37151#.V3pnhdIkpyc

Wang, Q. R., Dong, Y., Cui, Y., & Liu, X. (2001). Instances of soil and crop heavy metal contamination in China. *Soil and Sediment Contamination, 10*(5), 497–510.

Wang, X., Zhao, X. L., Zhang, Z. X., Yi, L., Zuo, L. J., Wen, Q. K., Liu, F., Xu, J., Hu, S., & Liu, B. (2016). Assessment of soil erosion change and its relationships with land use/cover change in China from the end of the 1980s to 2010. *Catena, 137*, 256–268. DOI: 10.1016/j.catena.2015.10.004

Wen, Q., Zhang, Z., Zhao, X., Yi, L., Wang, X., Hu, S., & Bin, L. (2015). Regularity and causes of grassland variations in China over the past 30 years using remote sensing data. *International Journal of Image and Data Fusion, 6*(4), 330–347.

Wong, E. (2014). One-fifth of China's farmland is polluted, state study finds. *The New York Times*. Retrieved 15 December 2016 from www.nytimes. com/2014/04/18/world/asia/one-fifth-of-chinas-farmland-is-polluted-state-report-finds.html?hpw&rref=science&_r=1

WWF Global. (2015). The Cradle of Chinese Civilization. WWF Global. Retrieved 15 December 2016 from http://wwf.panda.org/about_our_earth/about_freshwater/rivers/yellow_river/

Xiao, P. F., Li, H. X., Yang, Y. K., Wang, L. X., & Wang, X. H. (2015). Land-use changes in China during the past 30 years. In: Cui, X., Zhu, W., Xu, X., & Li, X. (Eds.) *Land-Use Changes in China: Historical Reconstruction Over the Past 300 Years and Future Projection.* Singapore: World Scientific, Ch. 2, pp. 11–28.

Xinhua. (April, 2014). China alerted by serious soil pollution. Xinhua News Agency. Retrieved from www.china.org.cn/environment/2014-04/17/content_32129341.htm

Yang, Z. F., Yu, T., Hou, Q. Y., Xia, X. Q., Feng, H. Y., Huang, C. L., Wang, L., Lv, Y., & Zhang, M. (2014). Geochemical evaluation of land quality in China and its applications. *Journal of Geochemical Exploration, 139,* 122–135. Retrieved from http://dx.doi.org/10.1016/j.gexplo.2013.07.014

Zhang, X. Y., Zhong, T. Y., Liu, L., & Ouyang, X. Y. (2015). Impact of soil heavy metal pollution on food safety in China. *PLoS One, 10*(8): e0135182. DOI: 10.1371/journal.pone.0135182

Zhang, Y. (August, 2014). Soil quality in China – Policy implications. Europe China Research and Advice Network (ECRAN). Short Term Policy Brief 98. Retrieved 15 December 2015 from https://pdfs.semanticscholar.org/1e4a/1c0ab49da926c85 8a7f99d0a81910b67f68a.pdf

Zhao, F. J., Ma, Y. B., Zhu, Y. G., Tang, Z., & McGrath, S. P. (2014). Soil contamination in China: Current status and mitigation strategies. American Chemical Society. *Environmental Science & Technology, 49*(2), 750–759.

3   The causes of soil degradation and soil pollution

Introduction

Soil is alive: just a handful of soil contains more microorganisms than the number of people who ever walked the Earth. These microbes decompose organic matter and support the resilience and health of the soil, which is fundamental to the circle of life on the planet. Carbon is an essential source of energy for microbes. Land that is disturbed is gradually depleted of its carbon stocks (World Economic Forum, 2012). Land degradation can be described as a drop in the quality or productivity of the land and may be caused by natural or anthropogenic processes.

Mechanisms leading to land degradation can be triggered by physical, biological, or chemical factors. Significant physical factors include structural decline leading to anaerobism, compaction, crusting, erosion, environmental pollution, desertification, and the depletion of natural resources. The underlying chemical processes involve salinization, leaching, acidification, a decrease in the cation exchange capacity, and a decrease in fertility. Among the biological processes are a reduction in total and biomass carbon, a decrease in land biodiversity, including the critical issue of the eutrophication of surface water, the contamination of groundwater, and the emission of trace gases (CO_2, CH_4, N_2O, NO_x) from terrestrial ecosystems to the atmosphere (Eswaran et al., 2001).

According to Deng and Li (2016), in addition to the natural processes contributing to land degradation, a disproportionate increase in population and urbanization and the excessive exploitation and improper use of natural resources have led to a decline in soil quality on 539.2 million ha of land, which makes up about 56.2 per cent of the total land area of China. Soil erosion accounted for 180 million ha, desertification for 33.4 million ha, soil salinization for 99.13 million ha, pasture degradation for 200 million ha, and soil pollution for 26.7 million ha of land. The area of land available for agricultural production is about 130 million ha, approximately 14 per cent of the total national land area (Deng and Li, 2016).

This chapter introduces the causes of soil degradation and soil pollution. It starts with the natural causes of soil degradation and then discusses the agricultural activities that led to a deterioration of the soil. The chapter then turns to soil pollution and introduces the different heavy metal pollutants before discussing the agricultural, industrial, and urban sources of soil pollution.

Causes of soil degradation

Soil erosion is one of the most important environmental and agricultural problems all over the world, and it is also the main contributor to soil degradation, inflicting damage to soil resources, impairing the flow of ecosystem services, and jeopardizing sustainability (Rao et al., 2015). Soil degradation is the combined result of natural factors (both climatic and topographic) and human activities (including unsustainable farming practices). Usually, the dominant factors are natural causes, with climate being the principal driving force behind soil degradation. However, poor water resource management also plays a promoting or inducing role. For these reasons, the most serious soil degradation affects the drylands.

"Drylands" refers to lands with limited water availability (LADA, 2010). The majority of the land area in China is situated in arid or semi-arid regions. China's drylands cover 444.6 million ha, approximately 45 per cent of the country's total land area. Most of the country's drylands are located in northern China, stretching across 12 provinces, municipalities, and autonomous regions (AR), namely Xinjiang Uyghur AR, Inner Mongolia AR, Ningxia AR, Qinghai, Gansu, Shaanxi, Shanxi, Hebei, Liaoning, Heilonggjiang, Jilin provinces, and Beijing. The area affected by land degradation grows by approximately 350,000 ha every year due to the combined effects of deforestation, unsustainable farming practices, and poor water resource management. LADA (2010) showed that one of the main contributors to soil degradation in China's dryland areas is a combination of its main climatic features, namely limited precipitation with a high annual variability, high evaporation, and frequent gales.

Drylands have an increased risk of drought and desertification because of their unique natural attributes, the first one being water scarcity. Although there is surface water in the form of rivers, lakes, and glaciers dispersed throughout China's drylands, the area suffers from insufficient water resources. While the dryland region of northwest China makes up over 40 per cent of the total land area, its water resources make up only 10 per cent of the total water available in China. As stated by LADA, the annual rainfall in the arid dryland region west of the Helan Mountains (apart from its highest mountain peaks) is less than 200 mm, while the desert and semi-desert regions such as the Gobi receive less than 10 mm of rain a year. The amount of annual rainfall in the semi-arid dryland regions ranges between 200 and 400 mm, with short-term heavy precipitation events in summer accounting for over 50 per cent of the total annual rainfall (LADA, 2010).

Apart from poor precipitation, drylands in China also have high evaporation rates. In most drylands, the amount of evaporation from water surfaces falls between 1,000 and 1,400 mm, and it can reach 2,200 to 2,400 mm in semi-arid lands such as the inner part of the Tarim Basin (LADA, 2010). In addition, winds are strong and frequent, especially in winter and spring. In an average year, most of the dryland areas of Inner Mongolia have over 50 days with force 8 winds; in the Junggar Basin, there are 50–75 days with force 8 winds, and the central part of the Qinghai-Tibet Plateau have more than 100 days with force 8 winds. In addition, the region suffers from poor water resource management, which further contributes to the deterioration of the land.

General conditions of soil degradation

Water erosion, wind erosion, and freeze-thaw erosion are the root causes of complex problems affecting China's degraded land. In China, the severity of soil degradation varies mainly between the classes of slight and moderate (Figure 3.1):

(1) Slight degradation. The degradation process is in its initial stage, and it is comparatively easier to restore the land. The vegetation cover is over 50 per cent.
(2) Moderate degradation. Degradation is more obvious, but it is possible to restore it. The vegetation cover is 50 per cent to 30 per cent.
(3) Severe degradation. There are obvious signs of degradation; the natural properties of the land have been changed considerably, and it is difficult to rapidly restore it. The vegetation cover is 30 per cent to 10 per cent.
(4) Extreme degradation. The vegetation cannot be restored. The vegetation cover is less than 10 per cent.

Figure 3.1 shows the types and severity of soil degradation in China. As can be seen, the greatest problems is wind erosion, which is responsible for over 50 per cent of the total soil erosion, including most of the severe and extremely severe land degradation. The second most important type of soil erosion is caused by freeze-thawing, because of the large area where

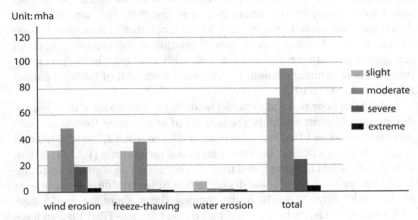

Figure 3.1 Types and severity of soil degradation (unit: million ha)
Source: LADA (2010)

this problem occurs. On the other hand, perhaps surprisingly, there is comparatively little water erosion. In China, slight land degradation makes up 36.8 per cent of the total affected area and moderate land degradation accounts for 48.3 per cent, while severe and extremely severe land degradation represents 12.6 per cent and 2.3 per cent, respectively, of the total area affected by land degradation (Figure 3.1) (LADA, 2010).

Wind erosion

The most dominant and critical type of soil degradation in China is erosion caused by wind. In particular in the semi-arid and arid lands of northern China, aeolian processes are the most significant causes of soil erosion. Wang (2014) points to two natural causes of wind erosion: (1) global warming and aridification processes in the middle latitude zones and (2) strong and frequent wind in areas characterized by dry climates and erratic rainfall. However, through self-regulation mechanisms, "when the system suffers from slight damage, it can be self-regulated by its internal feedback mechanism, thereby maintaining the stability of the system" (Tao, 2014: 36). Wang (2014) concludes that desertification due to natural causes occurs on a small scale, is of low severity, and is reversible.

In 2014, an assessment of aeolian desertification revealed that by 2010, the area of degraded soil affected by wind erosion amounted to 376 million ha, which accounts for approximately 44.1 per cent of the total land area affected by soil degradation in China (Guo et al., 2014). Approximately 80 per cent of the land eroded by wind is slightly or moderately degraded, which means that although the affected land area is large, most of these wind-eroded areas can be rehabilitated (LADA, 2010). Spatially, land degradation by wind most commonly occurs in the arid and semi-arid lands of northern China, extending from the Hulun Buir Sandy Land in northeast China to the Kashi City in Xinjiang AR, where the amount of annual precipitation is less than 500 mm (Guo et al., 2014).

Wind erosion has a great impact on the productivity of agricultural land. Impacts include sandblast damage to the crops, which result in reduced yield, and soil drifting, which reduces the fertility of the soil and gradually causes textural changes in the soil. The long-term consequence of wind erosion may be that the area becomes a desert and will be characterized by extreme aridity, desolation, rare vegetation, and lifelessness (LADA, 2010). In China, the Ministry of Environmental Protection (MEP) divides wind erosion into three classes according to their degree of severity (MEP, 2003). Table 3.1 shows the indicators of wind erosion in China including the affected areas, vegetation coverage, the characteristics of the landscape, and a decrease in the crop yield.

Table 3.1 Indicators of wind erosion severity

Degree	Wind erosion area (per cent)	Vegetation coverage (per cent)	Characteristics of the landscape	Decrease of land biological productivity (per cent)
Light	< 10	70~50	Spot-like distribution of quicksand or wind-eroded area. The height of sand dunes or shrub-coppice dunes is below 2 m; aeolian sand exists in some places.	10~30
Moderate	10~30	50~30	Comparably larger distribution of moving sand dunes with a height of 2–5 m; granule lands are distributed widely.	30~50
Severe	≥ 30	≤ 30	Dense distribution of moving sand dunes over 5 m in height.	≥ 50

Note: Figure 3.1 differentiates between "Severe" and "Extremely severe". This table brings together these two classes.

Source: MEP (2003)

Permafrost and soil freeze-thaw erosion

The term permafrost refers to the layer of soil that remains frozen for more than two consecutive years. Permafrost is easily affected by climatic stresses and human activities. When the weather becomes warmer, permafrost starts to thaw. When the temperature drops subzero again, the water in the soil leads to the formation of frost heaves. Frost heaves alter the structural arrangement of soil particles, changing the physical properties of the soil. Yang et al. (2004) argued that climatic stresses could lead to frequent and intense freeze-thaw processes in the active layer in frozen regions, with even multiple freeze-thaw cycles occurring on the same day. Studies have also shown that freeze-thaw erosion can increase soil erodibility and slope soil instability, thereby increasing water erosion: the precipitation occurring in early spring "often results in high rates of runoff and erosion on frozen soil due to its poor infiltration capacity" (Kong and Yu, 2013: 1). This process mostly occurs in colder climates at high latitudes and altitudes (Ran et al., 2012).

Permafrost areas in China are the third largest in the world (after Russia and Canada). The total area of permafrost in China is estimated at ~159 million ha (glaciers and lakes excluded) (Ran et al., 2012), while the second national soil erosion remote sensing survey estimated the freeze-thaw areas in China to total over 127 million ha, about 13.4 per cent of the entire country (Kong and Yu, 2013). Freeze-thaw erosion mainly takes place in the northwest, northeast, and on the Tibetan Plateau. According to the survey, the Tibetan Plateau, the source of the Yellow and Yangtze Rivers, has a freeze-thaw erosion area of 104 million ha (Kong and Yu, 2013). The by-products of freeze-thaw erosion have become some of the main components of sediments in the Yangtze and Yellow Rivers. About 30 per cent of the total area affected by freeze-thaw degradation is slightly eroded, and 36 per cent is moderately eroded (Figure 3.1) (LADA, 2010).

Water erosion

Water erosion is another type of land degradation process. Rain causes water erosion when it washes away the top layer of the soil, which exposes the underlying layers to the elements and lowers the quality of the soil, its structure and its physical stability, reducing the soil's water storage capacity. This also increases the amounts of carbon dioxide released by the soil. When heavy rains wash away the topsoil, the water also disturbs or removes the seeds, natural nutrients, pesticides, and fertilizers necessary for plant growth, directly affecting crop emergence, growth rate, and crop yield.

Lands affected by water erosion are mainly distributed in the Loess Plateau region, with the most severely affected parts in Dingxi City (Gansu

Table 3.2 Indicators of water erosion severity

Degree	Poor or rocky slope area (per cent)	Valleys (rill, cut ditch, gully) (per cent)	Vegetation coverage (per cent)	Characteristics of the landscape	Decrease of land biological productivity (per cent)
Light	< 10	< 10	70~50	Spot-like distribution of poor land or rocky slope. The depth of valleys is below 1 m; exposed sand surfaces are distributed sporadically	10~30
Moderate	10~30	10~30	50~30	Comparably larger distribution of poor land or rocky slopes; The depth of valleys is 1~3 m; exposed sand surfaces are distributed widely.	30~50
Severe	≥ 30	≥ 30	≤ 30	Dense distribution of poor land or rocky slopes; The depth of valleys is over 3 m.	≥ 50

Note: Figure 3.1 differentiates between "Severe" and "Extremely severe". This table brings together these two classes.

Source: MEP (2003)

Province), the southern part of Ningxia and Shaanxi Provinces, and the northern part of Shanxi Province (Zhao et al., 2015). The affected area is large and broad. Similarly to wind erosion, the MEP divides the degree of water erosion into three classes (Table 3.2)

There is a positive correlation between precipitation and the severity of water erosion. The Loess Plateau in particular experiences serious water erosion, partly because most of the precipitation comes in the form of heavy storms (LADA, 2010). Tsunekawa et al. (2014) argued that the main natural factors contributing to water erosion in the Loess Plateau are the concentrated, high-intensity rainstorm events. The average annual precipitation of the area is between 200 and 700 mm, but most of this water falls during the months of July, August, and September, which account for 50 per cent of the total annual precipitation in the region. Rainstorms during this period often start severe water erosion processes, increasing the levels of sediment concentration and its transportation to the Yellow River and its tributaries. For example, in 1977, the city of Yan'an (in Shaanxi Province) received 228mm of rain in just 30 minutes, which caused the flooding of the Yanhe River. The amount of sediment measured was five times the annual average. The most intense rainfall event ever observed was in Ordos, Wushenqi County, on 1 August 1997, when the precipitation reached 1410 mm over a 10-hour period (Tsunekawa et al., 2014). Han et al. (2016) found that water erosion affects more than 45 per cent of the region.

Another area with particularly high water erosion rates is Xinjiang Uyghur AR. Zhang et al. (2015b) showed that in 2011, the area affected by water erosion in Xinjiang Uyghur AR totaled 8.76 million ha, mainly located in the Ili River Valley and the northern and southern parts of the Tian Mountains. According to Zhang et al., tectonic uplift, topography, soil erodibility, rainfall, and the degradation of vegetation are the five most significant natural causes of water erosion in Xinjiang AR.

First, Xinjiang AR is a region that has been dominated by enhanced/intense sediment deposition since the late Permian period (about 260 million years ago), while the intense tectonic uplifts in the Himalayas also shaped the current landscape of the Tian Mountains. Tectonic uplift changes the base level of erosion and can contribute to soil erosion and deposition. The large amount of clastic rocks and deposition resulting from neo-tectonic uplift provides a material source for erosion.

Second, the average elevation of the Tian Mountains is around 4,000 m above sea level (ASL), 3,000 m higher than its Junggar and Tarim Basins (Zhang et al., 2015b). The slope gradient is one of the key factors affecting the intensity of soil erosion, especially in highland regions that are situated above 600 m ASL. Without plant cover, the intensity of soil erosion is aggravated on steep terrain, due to a drop in water infiltration rates, reduced water-holding capacity, and an increase in surface flow velocity (Lee et al., 2013). Kateb et al. (2013) compared the amount of eroded material and surface runoff across five plant covers and three different slope gradients (slight slope > 10°–≤ 20°, moderate slope > 20°–≤ 30°, and steep slope > 30°) and found that there is a positive correlation between slope angle and the amount of eroded material and runoff. Soil and water loss occurred in farmlands and grasslands with slopes of 3°–8° in the Ili River Valley, while the formation of landslides was observed in hills with slopes between 30°and 40°. The average slope of the Kahai watershed in the western part of the Tian Mountains was 18.5°, with a maximum value of 62.8°, which makes the formation of landslides more common in these places.

Third, the most common soil types in mountain areas are isohumosols and cambosols. Cambosols are soils with a less developed profile and a cambic horizon. In most cases, these soils are too shallow to absorb precipitation runoff and therefore have a tendency toward erosion. The last two factors are rainfall and vegetation degradation. The snow is relatively heavy in winter, and the surface runoff from melted snow can lead to flooding and erosion in spring. Although precipitation is generally limited in Xinjiang AR, isolated heavy rains may occur. Besides, the ecosystems of Xinjiang AR are particularly fragile because of the aridity of the region, resulting in a thin vegetation cover that is easily destroyed (Kateb et al., 2013).

Soil degradation due to agricultural and livelihood activities

Different types of vegetation affect the rates at which the soil can absorb rainfall. Forested areas have higher infiltration rates, meaning that precipitation in those areas causes less surface runoff, reducing the erosion of surface materials. In these areas, a substantial portion of the water runs into subsurface flows and generally has a low erosion potential. In forested systems, plant litter and shrub canopies protect the soil from the physical effects of rainfall, which is one of the main agents of erosion. The presence of vegetation can also slow down the accumulation of surface runoff by allowing more time for the water to infiltrate, thus facilitating high infiltration rates. Though natural factors also contribute to soil erosion, if the natural plant cover is destroyed, for example by the transformation of forestland into farmland, the process of soil erosion is accelerated.

According to the World Bank (2007), centuries of overuse and overgrazing have led China's Loess Plateau to experience one of the highest erosion rates in the world. Wang (2014) also argued that human activities, such as changing rangelands into farmlands, the overcultivation and overgrazing of lands, and excessive fuelwood collection have a much more severe impact on the soil than natural land degradation processes. Guo et al. (2014) also identified human activities as one of the key factors responsible for soil degradation: in the arid and semi-arid regions of northern China eroded by wind, the over-collection of fuelwood is responsible for 31.8 per cent of erosion, overgrazing for 28.3 per cent, overcultivation for 25.4 per cent, inappropriate irrigation for 8 per cent, and engineering construction for 1 per cent (Guo et al., 2014: 8954–8955).

Professor Mu Xingming of the Institute of Soil and Water Conservation named the Yellow River basin one of the areas worst affected by water erosion. He said, "Historically, it got its name because of its colour – because the water contains more mud and sand than other rivers. But now it's yellower because of human activities." Mu argued that more efforts should be made to rehabilitate degraded forests and grasslands and suggested that humans should completely abandon some of the degraded lands in order to allow them to recover (Branigan, 2008).

Overgrazing

Pastoral land covers about 400 million ha in China, making up about 41.7 per cent of the total land area. Home to the country's non-Han Chinese population, most of this pastoral land is located on the high plains in semi-arid regions dedicated to the production of meat, fur, wool, and cashmere. Intensive land use over the last century has caused different levels of pasture degradation on 90 per cent of this land, particularly in regions with more arid climates that have more vulnerable ecosystems (WLE, 2016).

The "co-developing area" is a belt of farming and pasture industries that runs through 12 provinces and autonomous regions from the northeast to the southwest. The area covers about 110 million ha and suffers from the most severe vegetation damage in China. *People's Daily* (2000) reported that

> overgrazing has caused the desertification of about 80 per cent of the 57.47 million ha of pasture in the co-developing area. The same thing is happening to the 51.9 million ha of farmland, where 45 per cent of the belt has been covered with sand.

In northwest China's Xinjiang Uygur AR, 40 per cent of the 57.3 million ha of grasslands have been severely degraded, and grass yields shrank by 30 to 50 per cent in 2011 (Xinhua, 2011). The Horqin Desert, Muus Desert, Tengger Desert, and Badain Jaran Desert are still growing by several thousand hectares every year (People's Daily, 2000).

The process of grazing-induced grassland degradation has three stages. Overgrazing initially results in a dramatic drop in biodiversity, plant cover, height of grass, and grass yield. Then, if the grazing pressure continues, perennial grasses begin to disappear, followed by palatable annual grasses, and eventually the grassland is overtaken by unpalatable or toxic grass species (Wang, 2014).

According to the grassland degradation data supplied by the Animal Husbandry Institute of the Chinese Academy of Agricultural Sciences and the desertification monitoring data of China, 48.2 per cent of grassland degradation and 37.44 per cent of forestland degradation were triggered by overgrazing (Nieuwenhuis, 2016). The rate of overgrazing in the areas affected by degradation ranges between 50–120 per cent and reaches 300 per cent in some places. At the same time, the trend of "less grass and more livestock" continues to worsen (LADA, 2010). One example is that of Maqu County (Gansu Province). According to the statistics of the Maqu County Animal Husbandry Department, in 1989 the county had a livestock count of 2,170,000 sheep units, with an overload of 350,000 sheep units (an overload rate of 19.2 per cent). In 1998, this overload had increased to 400,000 sheep units, although the actual numbers of livestock kept are probably further beyond the carrying capacity and reported statistics. To make the situation worse, herders from neighboring counties in Gansu and Qinghai provinces brought large numbers of animals to Maqu County for seasonal herding. A study of grassland degradation in the county indicates that the area affected by desertification grew from 4,798 ha in 1994 to 6,080 ha by 1999, with the affected area increasing by 256 ha, or 4.85 per cent, annually (LADA, 2010). In the Xillinggol Prefecture in Inner Mongolia, the number of livestock has increased from 2 million to 18 million between 1977 and 2000, desertifying one-third of its grassland area. Unless changes are implemented, the whole prefectural area could become unlivable by 2020 (Chakravarty et al., 2012).

In order to improve the degraded land, the central government is planning to complete a four-year relocation program targeting 1.2 million herders. Local authorities have also been imposing fines on Mongolian herders, forcing them to give up their pastoral lifestyle and be relocated into subsidized houses in resettlement villages established around urban areas (Roberts, 2015).

Plant harvesting for energy

In the majority of developing countries, wood is a principal energy source for people living in rural areas, and China is no exception. Despite the explosive growth of its economy over the last three decades, there are still many rural settlements in China in which biomass is the only source of energy for both heating and cooking. At the end of the 1990s, about two-thirds of rural settlements were still using biomass fuel, which made up about 60 to 71 per cent of total energy use in rural China at the time. According to Zhou et al. (2008), in northern China, 56 per cent of the total energy came from traditional biomass consumption in 1996. By 2005, this was still 47.2 per cent. According to official data, every year about 5.6 million ha of woodland is destroyed by the approximately 112 million rural people who have no other means for heating and cooking. "In 2001 alone, 171 tons of twig bundles – the equivalent of about 228 million cubic meters of timber – were burned by farmers throughout China, spelling a major consumption of the nation's forests" (China Daily, 2002).

Firewood harvesting is usually harmful to the surface vegetation as well as the surface soil: it "not only destroys local ecosystems, but also seriously pollutes the environment" (China Daily, 2002). The intensity of wind and water erosion processes are intensified by the sparse vegetation cover resulting from people's removal of trees. For example, LADA (2010) reports that the annual firewood consumption in the degraded land areas of Xinjiang AR (3.5–7 million tons) has brought about an enormous damage to the desert vegetation. In Hetian County of Xinjiang AR, the forestland area has been decreasing by 760 ha per year. So far, nearly two-thirds of the forest area in Xinjiang AR has been affected by sandification.

Collection of medicinal plants

In an effort to add to their income, some farmers/herdsmen dig and pick the local medicinal herbs, usually shoveling the soil and removing the grass, which seriously destroys grasslands and accelerates the process of land degradation. For example, according to officials of Inner Mongolia AR, over 100,000 farming herdsman from Gansu, Ningxia, and Inner Mongolia AR enter Alxa League (a prefecture-level division in Inner Mongolia AR) every year to dig Nostoc flagelliforme (发菜), inflicting serious damage to the grassland. It was estimated that 13 million ha of grassland of the Inner Mongolia AR have been damaged in recent years because of harvesting Nostoc flagelliforme, and over 4 million ha of this area have become sandified (LADA, 2010).

Similarly, in three counties of Ningxia AR (Yanchi, Tongxin, and Lingwu Counties), every year 7,000 ha of land become sandified due to the digging of *Glycyrrhiza uralensis* (甘草). Ma'erzhuang in Yanchi County (Ningxia AR) used to have a grassland area of 42,000 ha. However, with thousands of people digging the soil for *Glycyrrhiza uralensis*, a grassland area of 20,000 ha has been destroyed, and 33,300 ha of grazing land had become sandified land, almost destroying the entire grazing land of the area (LADA, 2010).

Causes of soil pollution

Contaminated soils with high amounts of heavy metals (for example cadmium [Cd], chromium (Cr), and lead [Pb]) can set off a phototoxic reaction in plants, decreasing crop yields. Moreover, the roots of plants can absorb these heavy metal pollutants, which accumulate in the crops and damage the health of the people who eat them. The bioaccumulation of heavy metals in the body can lead to severe health issues including abnormalities of the skeletal system, lung diseases, and cancers (Liu et al., 2016). Chapter 4 explores the health issues attributed to pollution in further detail.

According to a 2014 survey on the heavy metal and metalloid contamination of soil, in China, 16.1 per cent of the sampled land was contaminated by mercury (Hg), arsenic (As), cadmium, and lead; agricultural lands were primarily polluted by mercury, arsenic, cadmium, lead, copper (Cu), DDT, nickel (Ni), and polycyclic aromatic hydrocarbons; grasslands, forests, and unused lands were primarily affected by arsenic, cadmium, and nickel pollution. Cadmium ranked highest, with 7 per cent of the soil samples being

Table 3.3 Amount of land polluted with inorganic and organic pollutants

Pollutant	Per cent of land polluted	Degrees of exceedance (per cent)*			
		Light	Mild	Moderate	Severe
Inorganic pollutants					
Cadmium	7.0	5.2	0.8	0.5	0.5
Nickel	4.8	3.9	0.5	0.3	0.1
Arsenic	2.7	2.0	0.4	0.2	0.1
Copper	2.1	1.6	0.3	0.15	0.05
Mercury	1.6	1.2	0.2	0.1	0.1
Lead	1.5	1.1	0.2	0.1	0.1
Chromium	1.1	0.9	0.15	0.04	0.01
Zinc	0.9	0.75	0.08	0.05	0.02
Organic pollutants					
Dichlorodiphenyltrichloroethane	1.9	1.1	0.3	0.25	0.25
Polyaromatic hydrocarbons	1.4	0.8	0.2	0.2	0.2
Hexachlorocyclohexane	0.5	0.3	0.1	0.06	0.04

* Soil pollution is divided into five classes according to degree: soils with a pollutant level that does not exceed the quality standard are viewed as non-polluted; soils with levels that are not more than two times the maximum are viewed as being polluted lightly; soils with levels that are between two and three times the maximum are mildly polluted; soils with levels between three and five times the maximum are moderately polluted; and soils with levels that are more than five times the maximum are severely polluted (MEP, 2014) (see Chapter 1).

Source: MEP (2014)

polluted, followed by nickel (4.8 per cent), arsenic (2.7 per cent), copper (2.1 per cent), and mercury (1.6 per cent) (Table 3.3). Inorganic pollutants also exceed standards, although not to the extent of organic pollutants (Zhao et al., 2015).

Geographic distribution of heavy metals in soils

Zhang et al. (2016) emphasized the importance of calculating the amount, origin, and spatial distribution pattern of heavy metals in soils to establish quality standards for the different regions and estimate the potential impact of soil pollution on food safety and human health.

Distribution of cadmium in soils

Cadmium (Cd) is the most commonly found soil contaminant of all heavy metals in China. Li et al. (2016) argue that in the surface dust of cities, Cd mainly originates from tire wear, engine oils, coal combustion, waste treatment, the metal finishing industries, and the production and application of pesticides and fertilizers. Many provinces have Over Limit Sites (OLSs), but they are most prevalent in the provinces of Guizhou and Hunan and south of the Yangtze River. Field surveys conducted by Wang et al. (2016) in eight towns in Youxian (Hunan Province) showed that in 90 per cent of the study area the Cd content in the soil of rice paddies exceeded the permissible limit of 0.3 mg kg^{-1}, averaging 0.228–1.91 mg kg^{-1}. The highest distribution was found at Weining (Guizhou Province), home to the world's largest germanium mine. Cadmium OLSs were also found in Shandong, Henan, and Tianjin, all of which are densely populated regions with significant economic activities, as well as the Liaodong Peninsula in northeast China, a major heavy metal industrial region. The highest cadmium concentration (578 mg/kg, hundreds of times more than the allowed amount) can be found in the soils of Lanping County (Yunnan Province), close to the massive lead-zinc deposit in Jinding (Duan et al., 2016).

Distribution of lead in soils

High levels of lead (Pb) are another major threat to ecological and human health (Li et al., 2016). Sources of lead emission include engine oil, vehicle exhaust, tire wear, bearings, smelting, and oil products. Many cities in southern China are facing an acute lead contamination crisis. Two economically and demographically significant conurbations, Shanghai and Guangzhou, have particularly high concentrations of lead in their soil. Hezhang County in Guizhou Province, important for its lead and zinc mines, also shows dense lead OLSs. According to the available data, the highest density of lead in the soils in China (30,430 mg/kg) was found in Sanming, in close proximity to a lead and zinc smelting facility (Duan et al., 2016).

While fewer and lower density lead OLSs occurred in northern China than in southern and eastern China, there are still a number of places with relatively high concentrations. As an example, the Liaodong Peninsula in northeast China, as well as the strip of land between Chengxian (Gansu Province) and Xi'an (Shaanxi Province), has relatively high concentrations of lead OLSs. This is attributable to the geographical location of Chengxian, which sits in the prominent lead-zinc mineral belt of Xihe-Chengxian, where a massive mining zone has been excavated since the Ming Dynasty (Duan et al., 2016).

Distribution of zinc, arsenic, copper, and chromium in soils

According to Zhang et al. (2016), zinc (Zn), copper (Cu), and Cr concentrations were attributable to the soil's parent rocks and were also reflected by the spatial distribution of mineral surface structures, such as carbonates, organic matter, or clay. On the other hand, the high concentrations of lead (Pb), cadmium (Cd), and copper in the topsoil of agricultural lands were mostly due to human activities. While Zn, As, Cu, and Cr are scattered across the lands of China, they are not as densely distributed as cadmium or lead. The occurrence of zinc, arsenic, copper, and chromium Over Limit Sites (OLSs) is relatively rare.

Of the 1789 sites sampled for zinc, the vast majority of the 199 zinc OLSs were located in southern China. Many of the Zn OLSs are situated in the Yangtze River watershed, from Guizhou Province to Shanghai, forming a cluster in Hezhang and Weining counties (Guizhou Province) and Jishou (Hunan Province). In southern China, there are several Zn OLSs in the province of Fujian, especially in the cities of Sanming and Nanping, which are close to Pb and Zn mines and smelters. The situation of Xinxiang (Henan Province) is similar in this respect. The highest distribution of Zn OLSs was observed in Lanping County in Yunnan Province, with a Zn concentration of 49,210 mg/kg, which is 164 times as high as the standard Zn threshold limit value (Duan et al., 2016).

High arsenic (As) content in the soil is primarily attributable to arsenic-contaminated groundwater. Of the 1,339 sites included in the research, 70 arsenic OLSs were identified, primarily distributed in the north China Plain, especially in Tianjin Municipality and Jinan City (Shandong Province), with some others scattered across southern China. The largest As OLS is located in the city of Tongling along the bank of the Yangtze River, with a concentration of 2,300 mg/kg, which is 51 times as high as the standard maximum value of 45 mg/kg. In the region of the Pearl River basin, As OLSs were found around Hechi City (Guangxi Province) (Duan et al., 2016).

Of the 1997 copper sampling sites, 101 Cu OLSs have been identified. The majority of copper OLSs were located on the southeastern coast, forming a cluster in Guangzhou City. However, the largest copper OLS was found in Baoding City (Hebei Province), where the densest Cu concentration was 33,010 mg/kg, 165 times as high as the standard maximum value of 200 mg/kg (Duan et al., 2016).

Chromium is viewed as a serious environmental pollutant and is emitted by the steel, leather, and textile industries, among others (Zhang et al., 2016). Luckily, Cr OLSs are rare. The largest Cr OLS is located near Fuzhou (Fujian Province), with a Cr concentration reaching 875.59 mg/kg, about 2.5 times as high as the standard maximum value of 350 mg/kg. Zhang et al. (2016) estimated the risk that Cr in arable soil poses on food safety in China and concluded that agricultural practices should be suspended on 0.13 per cent of the arable land in the country due to their heavy Cr contamination, while 1.26 per cent of the soil faces a high risk of Cr pollution (Duan et al., 2016).

Soil pollution from agricultural activities

The rapid economic growth and urbanization over the last 30 years have brought about substantial changes in the diet of China's population. In particular, there has been a shift from the grain-centered diet toward a more diverse diet: the significant increase in incomes has created a demand for more animal protein, and high-quality vegetables and fruits. Between 1980 and 2002, the contribution of cereals and starchy roots to the average daily per capita calorie intake decreased by 17.4 per cent and 13.5 per cent, respectively. On the other hand, during the same period, the contribution of vegetables and fruits to people's diet increased by 260 per cent and 500 per cent, respectively (Chen, 2007).

Accordingly, soils previously used for cultivating crops like grains and starchy roots have been gradually transformed into lands for more high-value crops. Over the period of 1978–2014, the total land area used for cultivating grain crops dropped from 120.6 million ha to 112.7 million ha, while the land area used for oil-bearing crops increased from 6.2 to 14 million ha, that for vegetables increased from 3.3 to 21.4 million ha, and that for orchards increased from 1.6 to 13.1 million ha (an increase by 2.3 times, 6.5 times, and 8.2 times, respectively) (Figure 3.2) (Chen, 2007; NBSC, 2015).

Changes in food consumption habits and a market-oriented approach to agriculture in China have called forth the structural reorganization of the

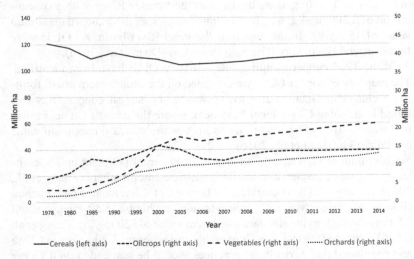

Figure 3.2 Change of land areas for different types of agricultural products (1978–2014)

Source: NBSC (2015)

country's agricultural system. Modifications in crop composition and crop yields fundamentally affect the way lands are utilized and managed, thereby also changing the capacity and nutrient cycles of soils. Different crop compositions require different nutrient supplies, as well as a specific balance of plant minerals applied to the soil, which also changes the physical and chemical properties of the soil. For example, the nutrient uptake of fruits and vegetables is significantly higher than that of cereal crops. Because vegetables have relatively underdeveloped root systems and an intensive growth and biomass accumulation period, they need a quicker soil nutrient release than cereals. On the other hand, oil-bearing crops need an ample supply of potassium (soybean kernels contain about five times more potassium than cereal crops).

These are some of the reasons underlying the high and growing levels of soil pollution generated by agricultural production. They lead, in particular, to the application of a growing amount of fertilizers and pesticides, the production of additional amounts of animal excretion, and the use of wastewater for irrigation. These issues are now discussed in turn.

Soil pollution by wastewater irrigation

Water sources in China are highly uneven, which results in an imbalanced water availability for irrigation. According to Lu et al. (2015), the Yangtze and Pearl River basins and the southeast and southwest river basins produce only 40 per cent of the total national grain yield, while over 70 per cent of the water resources can be found in these regions. On the other hand, about 50 per cent of the grain produced in China comes from the Songhua, Liaohe, and Haihe River basins in northern China, which only have 20 per cent of the water resources (China Water Risk, 2016). Figure 3.3 shows the mismatch between water resources and farmland in China's main agricultural provinces. The area with the greatest water scarcity in China is the north China Plain, which has 33.8 per cent of the national cropland but only 3.85 per cent of the country's water resources (Delang, 2016b).

The water scarcity in semi-arid and arid regions encourages water recycling. Since the 1950s, farmers have had to use urban and industrial wastewater (including sewage) to water their farmland, orchards, and vegetable gardens (Chen, 2007). Wastewater and sewage sludge is rich in nutrients such as nitrogen, phosphorus, and potassium; therefore, it can effectively improve the nutrient content of the soil to support crop growth (Bao et al., 2014). However, the use of untreated wastewater and sewage for irrigation can also increase the metal content in the soil and crops (including Cd, Pb, Cu, and Zn) (Cheng, 2003).

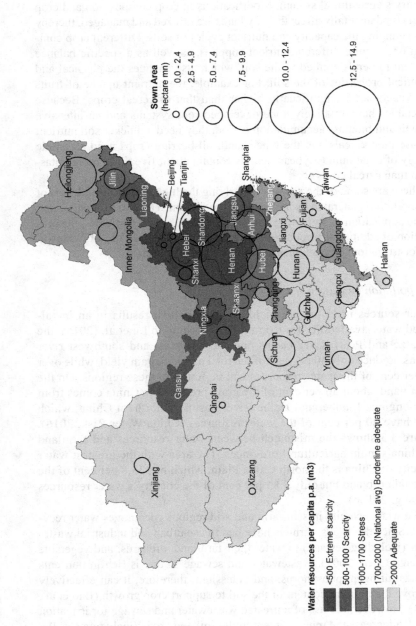

Sown Area (hectare mm)

- 0.0 - 2.4
- 2.5 - 4.9
- 5.0 - 7.4
- 7.5 - 9.9
- 10.0 - 12.4
- 12.5 - 14.9

Water resources per capita p.a. (m3)

- <500 Extreme scarcity
- 500-1000 Scarcity
- 1000-1700 Stress
- 1700-2000 (National avg) Borderline adequate
- >2000 Adequate

Figure 3.3 China's 2012 sown area mapped onto water resources

Source: Tan (2014)

In China, approximately one-third of the industrial effluent and over 90 per cent of the domestic sewage are discharged untreated into rivers and lakes. Nearly 80 per cent of China's cities (278 of them) have no wastewater treatment plants, and only a few of them plan to build one. A national survey revealed that in 1995, 3.62 million ha (about 1.6 times the affected area in the early 1980s) were irrigated by polluted water and sewage. This corresponded to 7.3 per cent of China's total irrigated area, or 10 per cent of the total land area irrigated with surface water. The area of lands directly irrigated with untreated urban sewage and industrial wastewater totaled 0.51 million ha (Chen, 2007). In general, surface water contamination affects northern China more seriously than southern China, particularly the regions of the Haihe River, Yellow River, and Huaihe River basins (Lu et al., 2015). On the other hand, about 40 per cent of China's agricultural land was irrigated with groundwater, of which 90 per cent was polluted, 60 per cent of it seriously (Qiu, 2010; Wee and Jourdan, 2013).

Tests showed that many crops are contaminated with heavy metals. As long as farmers continue to use untreated wastewater for irrigation, the contamination of the soils will continue, which will continue to damage crop quality and pose a direct threat to human health. In 2013, the government promulgated the "arrangement for soil environment protection and comprehensive treatment work" to prohibit the practice of using wastewater contaminated with heavy metals or persistent organic pollutants for irrigation (Lu et al., 2015). However, enforcing this rule is difficult, especially in northern China, due to the lack of good quality water. The authorities support farmers' efforts to drill deeper wells for irrigation, but this is only a temporary solution, while the original problem of polluting the rivers persists (China Water Risk, 2014). Lu et al. (2015) argue that the government devotes little attention to the potential long-term effects of wastewater irrigation and the resulting food safety issues. Since the public is not fully aware of the low quality of food stuffs, there are fewer pressures on the government to address the issue.

Soil pollution by overuse of fertilizers

Even though the overuse of fertilizers leads to soil contamination and food safety issues, agriculture in China largely relies on the use of chemical fertilizers (Yang, 2012). Yang and Fang's (2015) survey in five counties in east-central China to examine farmers' fertilizer application practices showed that 74 per cent of the farmers in Shandong Province and 47 per cent of the farmers in Shanxi Province have explained their increasing use of synthetic fertilizers with the decreasing use of organic fertilizers and having to offset the decline in soil fertility. Furthermore, to keep inflation in check, the

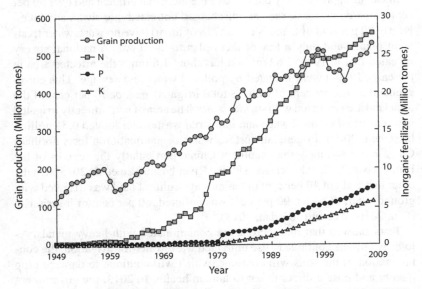

Figure 3.4 Crop production and synthetic fertilizer consumption in China (1949–2008); N = nitrogen, P = phosphate, K = potassium

Source: Sun et al. (2012)

government has been imposing profit caps on farmers. As a result, many farmers have been struggling to make a living, which forces them to increase their crop yields through greater use of synthetic fertilizers.

As depicted in Figure 3.4, the country's use of synthetic fertilizers has been steadily growing since the early 1960s, to meet the food demand of a huge population with a comparatively small agricultural area. According to Chinese Vice Minister of Agriculture Zhang Taolin, chemical fertilizer use has increased by 5.2 per cent a year over the last three decades (Patton, 2015). By 2008, the country's total fertilizer consumption amounted to 52 million tons, which is more than one-third of the global consumption of fertilizers. Despite these efforts, the growth rate of agricultural output has been slowing down since the 1990s (Sun et al., 2012).

Nitrogen (N), phosphate (P), and potassium (K) fertilizers are the three main chemical fertilizers used in China. According to Liu (2014), they are often applied in the proportion of 1:0.5:0.5, and internationally recognized limit for their maximum safe usage is between 225 kg per ha (CCICED, 2006) and 250 kg per ha (Liu, 2014). In China the amount applied is much larger: in 2011–2012, over 400 kg of fertilizers were applied per ha, according to Chen (2014); 480 kg per ha, according to Liu (2014); 516 kg per ha, according to Lu et al. (2015); and 647.6 kg per ha, according to the World Bank (Patton, 2015). Not all provinces apply the same amount of fertilizers. According to Liu (2014), the southeastern part of China has significantly higher fertilizer application rates than the northwestern part of the country. Fertilization rates in Fujian, Guangdong, Henan, Hubei, and Jiangsu exceed 690 kg ha^{-1}. The highest fertilization rate, about 908.7 kg ha^{-1}, was found in Fujian.

Nitrogen fertilizers are by far the most common (Figure 3.4), and China has become the world's largest producer and consumer of synthetic N fertilizer (Smil, 2013). The national average annual amount of nitrogen fertilizer use reached 230 kg N ha^{-1} in croplands, which is the third largest in the world after Korea and Japan. Data from the Soil and Fertilizer Institute of the Chinese Academy of Agricultural Sciences (CAAS) reveal that the average levels of N fertilizer consumption exceed the internationally set threshold in half of the Chinese regions (Yang, 2012). In some provinces, the average N fertilizer use exceeds 400 kg ha^{-1} (in Guangdong Province it is 448.5 kg ha^{-1}, Figure 3.5), and in some counties with vegetable farms it is over 1,000 kg ha^{-1} (Sun et al., 2012).

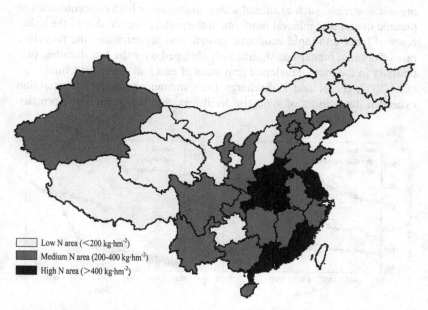

Figure 3.5 Provincial differences in N fertilizer use intensity

Source: Liu (2014)

The highest application rates of phosphate fertilizer, about 259.8 kg ha^{-1}, were found in Henan, while the highest application rates of potassium fertilizer, about 264.73 kg ha^{-1}, were found in Fujian (Liu, 2014).

Besides fertilizer overuse, there is also misuse. Since the 1980s, the effectivity rate of fertilizer application has been decreasing. According to Yang, "Only about 30 per cent of the fertilizers China uses actually does any good, much lower than the 40 per cent rates in western nations." A survey carried out by the agricultural authorities in Henan Province found that "only one-third of the three million tons of fertilizer used in the province was actually absorbed by crops" (Yang, 2012). A nationwide survey of pollution sources in 2007 showed that the total nitrogen loss from cropland was about 1.6 million tons, of which some 320,000 tons was from surface runoff and over 200,000 tons from underground leaching. The total phosphorus loss was of about 108,000 tons (Sun et al., 2012).

Soil pollution by waste from livestock

Intensive animal farming has spread rapidly across China over the last decades (Figure 3.6), resulting in the production of substantial amounts of waste (Sun et al., 2012). Chinese farmers used to recycle and compost organic materials, such as animal waste, to guarantee high concentrations of organic matter and mineral nutrients in the soil. However, due to the rising costs of labor and rapid economic growth and urbanization, the recycling rate of organic matter has significantly dropped over the last decades, particularly in the more developed provinces of east and southeast China.

In 2007, the N and P discharge from human and livestock excretion exceeded the amount of synthetic fertilizers, and has become the primary

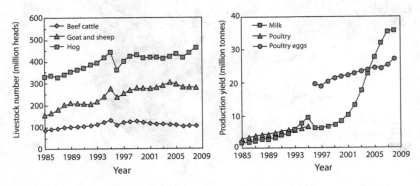

Figure 3.6 Livestock numbers and milk and poultry production (1996–2008)

Source: Sun et al. (2012)

source of non-point source (NPS) pollution in China. In 2007, livestock and poultry farming generated 243 million tons of waste and 163 million tons of urine; the amount of N and P discharged from animal excretion totaled 1,024,800 and 160,400 tons, respectively. Unfortunately, the majority of livestock are kept by small farmers who ignore waste discharge regulations: 90 per cent of animal farms in China have no or inadequate waste disposal or treatment plants. Ignoring the guidelines for the safe handling and storage of waste causes serious contamination (Ju et al., 2005).

Organic manure makes up only 35 per cent of the total amount of fertilizers applied to the land (Ju et al., 2005). However, organic fertilizers are not safe either. Huang Hongxiang, a researcher at CAAS's Institute of Agricultural Resources and Regional Planning, points out that even though chemical fertilizers pollute the land and the environment, lower the quality of the soil, and affect the taste of crops, they are not toxic themselves. According to the researcher, organic fertilizers derived from animal excrements are the real cause for concern. The reason behind this is that in the past, chickens and pigs used to be grain-fed, whereas now "pig fodder might contain antibiotics and hormones, while chicken fodder can contain a range of chemicals" that can pollute the soil when their manure is used to fertilize crops (Yang, 2012).

Increasing use of pesticides

For over 10 years, China has been the largest buyer of pesticides in the world, with the average amount of pesticides applied per unit area being double the global average (Sun et al., 2012). In 2000, organochlorine and organophosphorus pesticides made up over 39.4 per cent and 37.0 per cent of the total pesticide use, respectively, and the highly toxic organophosphorus and aminoformin pesticides made up 67.0 per cent of the total amount of insecticides used. These pesticides are primarily sprayed on vegetables, fruit bearing trees, and cereal crops (rice and wheat). The utilization of pesticides has significantly boosted China's agricultural productivity (Lu et al., 2015). According to Zhang et al. (2011), during the growing process, 78 per cent of fruits, 54 per cent of vegetables, and 32 per cent of cereals would be lost without the use of pesticides. Overall, the use of pesticides in China has prevented the loss of 89.44 million tons of cereals, 1.65 million tons of cotton, 2.53 million tons of oilseeds, and 78 million tons of vegetables.

However, pesticides are also highly toxic, and beyond a certain amount, they no longer help to boost agricultural output. Instead, they end up in the soil and water in amounts that exceed the ability of the natural environment to absorb, dilute, and decompose them. According to Zhang et al. (2011), only about 1 per cent of these toxic substances does any good, while the other 99 per cent will reach non-target soils and contaminate the water bodies and the atmosphere to eventually get absorbed by other living organisms.

According to China Water Risk (2014), aware of the problems caused by excessive use of fertilizers, pesticides, and wastewater for irrigation, farmers sell their contaminated crops in the market and buy their own food, or reserve a portion of land for their own personal use, on which they do not apply these chemicals.

Soil pollution from industrial activities

The extensive mining and smelting with poor environmental standards over the last decades has resulted in large amounts of heavy metal contaminants affecting farmlands through atmospheric deposition, waste transportation, and irrigation with wastewater and sludge. This problem has been particularly important in southern China, which contains large mineral deposits (Lu et al., 2015).

Soil pollution from coal mining

Coal is the most abundant energy resource in China. China's 12th Five-Year Plan (2011–2015) proposed the construction of 16 large coal power stations to meet the country's huge demand for energy. Unfortunately, coal power production is a water-intensive operation, and most coal mines are found in the drier areas in the north of the country (Figure 3.7). The coal reserves in the dryland areas in Inner Mongolia AR, Ningxia AR, and Shaanxi Province are estimated to amount to 250 billion tons. The coal reserve of Xinjiang AR comprises 35 per cent of the total coal reserves of the country. In these areas, coal competes with agriculture for water. Figure 3.7 shows the distribution of coal mines in China and the local precipitation. Inner Mongolia, which is China's largest coal-producing area, possesses 26 per cent of China's coal reserves but only 1.6 per cent of its water (Greenpeace, 2012).

The exploitation of coal supplies brings serious ecological problems (LADA, 2010). Surface mining (also known as open cast, mountaintop, or strip mining) involves removing the top layers of the soil and rocks to dig the coal closer to the surface. In many cases, "mountains may be blasted apart to reach thin coal seams within, leaving permanent scars on the landscape as a result" (Greenpeace, 2016). According to Greenpeace, surface mining devastates landscapes, woodlands, and wildlife habitats when the vegetation and topsoil are destroyed and cleared. This destructive practice results in soil erosion and the ruination of arable land. Although coal companies need to submit sound mine reclamation plans before starting their mining activities, the rehabilitation of water supplies, ecosystems, and air quality is a long and difficult process. In particular, re-seeding the native vegetation is challenging

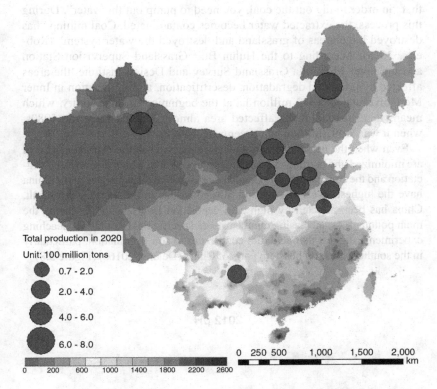

Total production in 2020
Unit: 100 million tons

- 0.7 - 2.0
- 2.0 - 4.0
- 4.0 - 6.0
- 6.0 - 8.0

0   200   600   1000   1400   1800   2200   2600

0   250 500   1,000   1,500   2,000
km

Figure 3.7 Major coal-mining bases under the 12th Five-Year Plan (shades of gray indicates annual precipitation, mm/a)

Source: Greenpeace (2012)

due to the extensive damage inflicted on the soil during the mining. Worse still, if a coal mining company goes bankrupt, the expensive mine reclamation process may not be completed. According to a 2004 estimate, coal mining in China devastated 3.2 million ha of land but only 10–12 per cent of the degraded land area was rehabilitated (Sun et al., 2012).

Underground coal mines can cause subsidence when a mine collapse occurs and the surface land starts to shift downwards. On average, 0.2 ha of land sinks per 10,000 t of mined coal. Subsidence also results in massive amounts of soil and waste rock being exposed to the surface, some of which may be toxic and come into contact with soils (Sun et al., 2012).

About 73.5 per cent of Inner Mongolia's grasslands already suffers from land degradation, and open-pit coal mining has only worsened the desertification process. Deng Ping, a campaigner for Greenpeace China, pointed out that "in order to dig out the coal, you need to pump out the water". During this process, the extracted water becomes contaminated. Coal mining "has destroyed huge areas of grassland and destroyed the water system" (Roberts, 2015). According to the Hulun Buir Grassland Supervision Station and the Inner Mongolia Grassland Survey and Design Institute, the areas affected by grassland degradation, desertification, and salinization in Inner Mongolia totaled 3.982 million ha at the beginning of this century, which means that the size of the affected area almost doubled since the 1980s, when it was 2.097 million ha (Greenpeace, 2012).

Even when the negative environmental impacts from the extraction of coal are minimized, the burning of coal causes air pollution, which degrades the vegetation and the soil. Chen (2007) argued that high coal burning rates made China have the highest levels of soot and SO_2 emissions in the world. As a result, China has been affected by high acid deposition levels, with SO_2 being the main pollutant. An increasing number of site-specific field studies and leaching experiments suggest that acid rain contributes to soil degradation, particularly in the southern and southeastern parts of China (Delang, 2016a) (Figure 3.8).

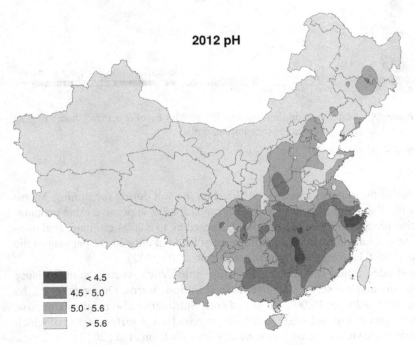

Figure 3.8 Annual average pH values of precipitation in China in 2012

Source: Tang and Wu (2012)

Pollution by industrial emission

Industrial emissions are a significant source of air pollution. When the airborne toxic chemicals and heavy metals fall back to the ground, they pollute the soil. Industrial emissions are some of the major sources of heavy metal pollution in China. While the concentration of cadmium (Cd) in the atmosphere is relatively low (usually below 1.0 pg/L) in rural areas without industrial activities, industrial areas show significantly higher values, reaching up to 100 pg/L. Soils in industrial areas can absorb Cd from the air and through precipitation. As a large agricultural country, China also produces large quantities of mercury (Hg) emissions from biomass burning (Huang et al., 2011). Biomass burning includes the outbreak of open fires (such as forest and grassland fires, and crop residue burning in fields) and biofuel combustion (such as crop residues and wood used as fuel).

Greenpeace has examined official statistics to conclude that the iron and steel industries are the largest contributors to cadmium and lead pollution in China, but there is also a considerable overlap between regions producing non-ferrous metals and crop producing areas (Greenpeace East Asia, 2014). Table 3.4 shows the top ten provinces producing non-ferrous metals. Among them, Inner Mongolia, Shandong, Henan, Jiangxi, Hunan, and Xinjiang AR are also major grain crop producers (Figure 3.3).

Soil pollution from urbanization

Urbanization is one of the major social trends affecting the planet. China has a relatively low level of urbanization. However, being the country with the largest population, it is also home to the world's largest urban population

Table 3.4 Top ten non-ferrous metal producing
provinces in China in 2015

No.	Province	Output (tons)
1	Shandong	9,182,036
2	Xinjiang	6,014,419
3	Henan	5,213,468
4	Gansu	3,813,625
5	Inner Mongolia	3,403,519
6	Yunnan	3,328,341
7	Hunan	2,674,557
8	Qinghai	2,306,090
9	Shannxi	2,006,890
10	Jiangxi	1,677,993

Source: Cnal (2016)

(Chen, 2007). Starting with the economic reform of 1978, China experienced a dramatic increase in urban population, from 17.9 per cent to around 55 per cent of its population by 2015 (Steinbock, 2010). The rapid urbanization, along with the rapid economic growth over the last three decades, has exacerbated the problem of agricultural land scarcity and soil pollution in China.

First, urbanization withdraws the best land from cultivation. Cities have historically been formed near the most fertile lands. When the cities expand, the new buildings are built on that farmland. Urbanization has contributed to the growth rate in agricultural output slowing down since the 1990s (Figure 3.4).

Second, as pollution is concentrated, it cannot dilute to levels that are manageable by the natural environment. Soil pollution problems are much more severe in ecological deficit areas and in densely inhabited conurbations because of the concentration of pollutants. For example, crudely disposing of sewage and waste from a big city creates water or land pollution. However, the same number of people and the same volume of sewage might not create a problem if it were created in 10 smaller cities or 100 small towns. The same is true for acid deposition caused by the high concentration of pollutants emitted in cities.

China's ecological footprint (people's impact on the ecosystem) has been steadily increasing over the years, while the biocapacity (the capacity of the productive land to provide resources as well as to eliminate waste) has been gradually decreasing. In the 1960s, China's ecological footprint per capita was about 1 gha (global hectares, which represents the productive capacity of one hectare of available land at global average biological productivity levels), about the same as its biocapacity (Figure 3.9). At that time, China's economy could be said to have been sustainable. By 2012, China's ecological footprint per capita reached 3.38 gha, while its biocapacity had dropped to 0.94 gha as a result of environmental degradation. In 2012 the per capita ecological footprint was 3.6 times higher than the available biocapacity (Footprintnetwork, 2016). However, the situation is worse in its largest urban areas. In 2009, the per capita ecological footprint in Shanghai and Beijing was about 4 gha, which was 13 times larger than the local biocapacity. For comparison, during the same year, the biocapacity of Yunnan province exceeded its ecological footprint (WWF, 2014).

The disposal of waste did not always lead to soil contamination. In past centuries, people primarily used natural materials (coming from plants, animals, or the minerals found in the soil); therefore, the waste and by-products were mostly organic (carbon-based) and would gradually decompose. However, during the 20th century, new types of synthetic materials, such as plastics and composites, have been invented, which the environment takes much longer to decompose. For instance, it can take up to 500 years for plastic to

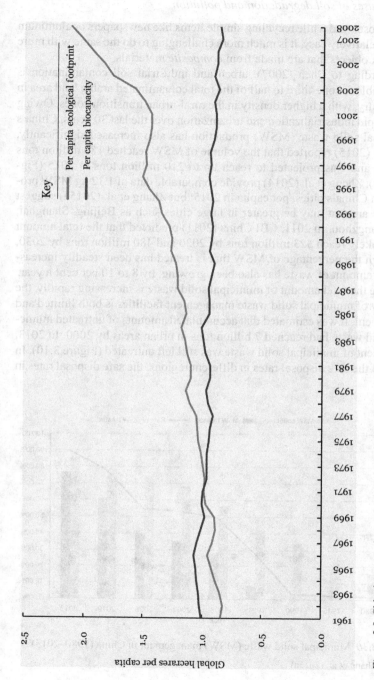

Figure 3.9 China's per capita ecological footprint and biocapacity (1961–2008)

Source: Footprintnetwork (2016)

decompose. And while recycling simple items like newspapers or aluminum cans is relatively easy, it is much more challenging to do the same with more complex objects that are made from *composite* materials.

According to Chen (2007), urban and industrial soil contamination is responsible for one-third to half of the total contaminated arable land area in the country, with a higher density in the rural-urban transition zones. Owing to the rapid industrialization and urbanization over the last 30 years, China's municipal solid waste (MSW) production has also increased significantly. Fu et al. (2015) reported that the volume of MSW reached 180 million tons in 2010 and was projected to reach up to 210 million tons in 2015 (Figure 3.10). Zheng et al. (2014) provide comparable data of 1.12 kg MSW produced in China's cities, per capita in 2015; but Zhang et al. (2015a) suggest that this amount may be greater in large cities such as Beijing, Shanghai, and Guangzhou. In 2011, CBI China (2011) predicted that the total amount would likely reach 323 million tons by 2020 and 480 million tons by 2030. Although the percentage of MSW that is treated has been steadily increasing, the amount of waste has also been growing, by 8 to 10 per cent a year.

While the total amount of municipal solid waste is increasing rapidly, the capacity of municipal solid waste management facilities is both limited and insufficient. It was estimated that accumulated amounts of untreated municipal solid waste had reached 7 billion tons in urban areas by 2000. In 2013, 10 per cent of municipal solid waste was still left untreated (Figure 3.10). In terms of the safe disposal rates in different regions, the safe disposal rates in

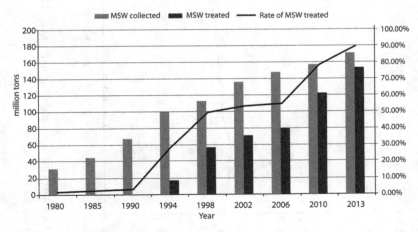

Figure 3.10 Municipal solid waste (MSW) management in China (1980–2013)

Source: Zhang et al. (2015a)

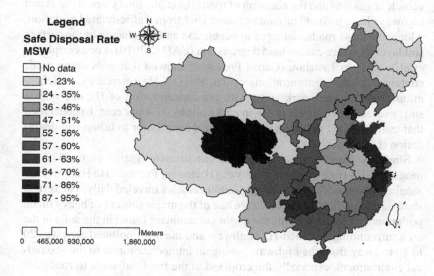

Figure 3.11 Safe disposal rates of municipal solid waste (MSW) at the provincial level (2007)

Source: Chen et al. (2010)

coastal regions (Beijing, Shanghai, and the provinces of Tianjin, Shandong, Fujian, Jiangsu, Zhejiang) and western regions (Qinghai, Sichuan, Guizhou, Yunnan, and Shaanxi) are higher than in the central inland regions (Shanxi, Henan, Anhui, Hunan, and Hubei) (Figure 3.11) (Chen et al., 2010). Severe soil contamination not only occurs at and around garbage disposal sites, which occupy an estimated total area of over 55,000 ha in China, but also in the extensive rural-urban transition zones where municipal solid waste landfills are under little control (Chen, 2007).

Road construction and vehicle pollution

With the rapid development of the economy, automobiles have become more affordable. As a result, traffic-related pollution has developed into a significant contributor to urban environmental degradation and public health problems (Li et al., 2007). While road construction may lead to soil erosion, the traffic itself contributes to the accumulation of heavy metals. Many studies showed that traffic-related pollution can result in the accumulation of some heavy metals such as Pb (lead), Cd (cadmium), Zn (zinc), and Cu in both the soil and plants along roads, primarily attributable to vehicle emissions and the abrasion of roads (Li et al., 2007). Some roads and highways have a "belt" of contaminated land from traffic-related pollution. Alongside these roads, damages to vegetation and the change of the surface soil layer structure causes land degradation (LADA, 2010). For example, Li et al.'s study in Lanzhou (Gansu Province) showed that soils along roads contained higher concentrations of Zn, Pb, Cd, Hg (mercury), Cr (chromium), and Cu than park soils, with the concentration of Hg in roadside soils exceeding the levels of Hg in park soils by 71.4 per cent. Li concluded that traffic-related pollution is a significant contributor to urban soil degradation (Li et al., 2007).

Similarly, Han et al. (2009) carried out an investigation on the 532 km long Shen-Ha Highway from Shenyang (Liaoning Province) to Harbin (Heilongjiang Province), where about 50,000 vehicles traveled daily. The results showed that vehicle emissions were one of the major sources of heavy metal pollution in the area. Pb was the major contaminant found in the soils in the area surrounding the Shen-Ha Highway, and the most polluted area was 20 to 40 m away from the highway, posing an immediate threat to the ecological environment, especially the cropland in the fields adjacent to roadsides (Han et al., 2009).

Conclusion

Concerns have been growing nationwide over the issues of soil degradation and the availability of arable land. In late 2013, a national soil survey published by China's Ministry of Land and Resources reported that the area of lands suitable for cop production was gradually decreasing due to soil degradation, pollution, and urbanization. The survey revealed that between 2006 and 2009, 0.2 per cent of China's arable land had become degraded due to these processes, and 2.5 per cent of the land was declared unfit for farming due to the presence of heavy metals and other contaminants (He, 2014).

The state of soil erosion and soil pollution raise deep concerns in China, especially because China has little agricultural land per capita. Natural factors play an important role in the soil degradation process since many areas are prone to water erosion, wind erosion, and freeze-thaw erosion. However, human activities, especially farming, also accelerate the process of soil erosion. Soil erosion is particularly important in northern China, where there is little precipitation. In these areas, the lack of rain prevents farmers from growing crops and reduces the economic opportunities available to pastoralism, which itself degrades the land and is very destructive to the remaining grassland. The impacts are felt beyond the region, in particular in the form of dust storms that can reach Beijing and even as far as Korea and Japan.

On the other hand, soil pollution is mainly attributable to human activities. One of the constraints that have led to soil pollution is the problem of water scarcity. Farmers solve this problem by applying industrial wastewater and urban sewage, which pollutes the soil and has direct consequences on the quality of the food grown. In addition, farmers apply large amounts of fertilizers and pesticides, well beyond what is necessary to grow food and kill pests. This increases soil pollution and gradually leads to soil degradation. From the perspective of farming, there is also the problem of pollution from livestock waste, which contains considerable amounts of antibiotics. In addition to the detrimental practices of farmers, sources of soil pollution include the general processes of industrialization and urbanization, which indirectly result in soil pollution through the deposition of air pollutants.

The next chapter will discuss the impact of soil degradation and soil pollution, and Chapter 5 the policies that the government is pursuing to address the problems. As this chapter has hinted at, soil pollution is more difficult to address than soil degradation because the causes of soil pollution are diverse and are closely related to the production of food or the industrial activities that form the backbone of the Chinese economy.

Bibliography

Bao, Z., Wu, W. Y., Liu, H. L., Chen, H. H., & Yin, S. Y. (2014). Impact of long-term irrigation with sewage on heavy metals in soils, crops, and groundwater: A case study in Beijing. *Polish Journal of Environmental Studies*, 23(2), 309–318.

Branigan, T. (November, 2008). Soil erosion threatens land of 100m Chinese, survey finds. *The Guardian*. Retrieved 15 December 2016 from www.theguardian.com/world/2008/nov/21/china-soil-erosion-population

CBI China. China waste to energy outlook 2011: Updating technology and management, powering up the low-carbon economy. *CBI China*. Retrieved 15 December 2016 from http://events.cbichina.com/con/wte2011/index.html

CCICED. (2006). Environmental Issues and Countermeasures Facing New Rural Development in China. China Council for International Cooperation on Environment and Development. Retrieved 15 December 2016 from www.china.com.cn/tech/2008-02/03/content_9642876.htm

Chakravarty, S., Ghosh, S. K., Suresh, C. P., Dey, A. N., & Shukla, G. (2012). Deforestation: Causes, effects and control strategies. In: Okia, C. A. (Ed.) *Global Perspectives on Sustainable Forest Management*. Rijeka (Croatia): Intech, Ch. 1, pp. 1–26.

Chen, J. (2007). Rapid urbanization in China: A real challenge to soil protection and food security. *Catena*, 69(1), 1–15.

Chen, N. (December, 2014). *Chemical Fertilizer Overuse Linked to Land Degradation in China*. Beijing: Chinese Academy of Sciences. Retrieved 15 December 2016 from http://english.cas.cn/newsroom/china_research/201412/t20141226_133647.shtml

Chen, X. D., Geng, Y., & Fujita, T. (2010). An overview of municipal solid waste management in China. *Waste Management*, 30(4), 716–724. DOI: 10.1016/j.wasman.2009.10.011

64   *Causes of soil degradation and pollution*

Cheng, S. (2003). Heavy metal pollution in China: Origin, pattern and control. *ESPR – Environmental Science & Pollution Research, 10*(3), 192–198.
China Daily. (October, 2002). China boosts clean energy project in rural areas. Retrieved 15 December 2016 from www.china.org.cn/english/scitech/45590.htm
Chinamaps. (2016). China Climate Map: Annual Average Precipitation. Chinamaps. org. Retrieved 15 December 2016 from www.chinamaps.org/china/china-map-of-precipitation.html
China Water Risk. (April, 2014). Crying Lands: China's Polluted Waterscape. China Water Risk. Retrieved 15 December 2016 from http://chinawaterrisk.org/interviews/crying-lands-chinas-polluted-waterscape/
China Water Risk. (2016). Top 4 Farmers. China Water Risk. Retrieved 15 December 2016 from http://chinawaterrisk.org/big-picture/top-4-farmers/
Cnal. (March, 2016). Main nonferrous metal producing provinces in China in 2015: China nonferrous metals (in Chinese). Retrieved 15 December 2016 from https://news.cnal.com/2016/03-01/1456801860427801.shtml
Davison, N. (2013). China's taste for pork serves up a pollution problem. *The Guardian*. Retrieved 15 December 2016 from www.theguardian.com/world/2013/jan/01/china-taste-pork-pollution-problem
Delang, C. O. (2016a). *China's Air Pollution Problems*. London: Routledge.
Delang, C. O. (2016b). *China's Water Pollution Problems*. London: Routledge.
Deng, X., & Li, Z. (2016). Economics of land degradation in China. In: Nkonya, E., Mirzabaev, A., & Braun, J. von (Eds.) *Economics of Land Degradation and Improvement: A Global Assessment for Sustainable Development*. Heidelberg: Springer, Ch. 13, pp. 385–399.
Duan, Q. N., Lee, J. C., Liu, Y. S., Chen, H., & Hu, H. Y. (June, 2016). Distribution of heavy metal pollution in surface soil samples in China: A graphical review. *Bulletin of Environmental Contamination and Toxicology, 97*(3), 303–309. DOI: 10.1007/s00128-016-1857-9
Eswaran, H., Lal, R., & Reich, P. F. (2001). Washington: United States Department of Agriculture. Land Degradation: An overview. Retrieved 15 December 2016 from www.nrcs.usda.gov/wps/portal/nrcs/detail/soils/use/?cid=nrcs142p2_054028
Footprintnetwork. (2016). Public Data Package. Global Footprint Network. Retrieved 15 December 2016 from www.footprintnetwork.org/en/index.php/GFN/page/public_data_package
Fu, Z., Zhang, S., Li, X., Shao, J., Wang, K., & Chen, H. (2015). MSW oxy-enriched incineration technology applied in China: Combustion temperature, flue gas loss and economic considerations. *Waste Management, 38*, 149–156.
Greenpeace. (August, 2012). Thirty Coal: A Water Crisis Exacerbated. Greenpeace East Asia. Retrieved 15 December 2016 from www.greenpeace.org/eastasia/publications/reports/climate-energy/2012/thirsty-coal-water-crisis/
Greenpeace. (April, 2014). "Cadmium Rice": Heavy Metal Pollution of China's Rice Crops. Greenpeace East Asia. Retrieved 15 December 2016 from www.greenpeace.org/eastasia/publications/reports/toxics/2014/cadmium-rice-heavy-metal/
Greenpeace. (July, 2016). About Coal Mining Impacts. Greenpeace International. Retrieved 15 December 2016 from www.greenpeace.org/international/en/campaigns/climate-change/coal/Mining-impacts/

Guo, Z. L., Huang, N., Dong, Z. B., Van Pelt, R. S., & Zobeck, T. M. (2014). Wind erosion induced soil degradation in Northern China: Status, measures and perspective. *Sustainability*, *6*, 8951–8966. DOI: 10.3390/su6128951

Han, D. C., Zhang, X. K., Tomar, V. V. S., Li, Q., Wen, D. Z., & Liang, W. J. (2009). Effects of heavy metal pollution of highway origin on soil nematode guilds in north Shenyang, China. *Journal of Environmental Sciences*, *21*(2), 193–198. DOI: 10.1016/S1001–0742(08)62250–0

Han, F., Ren, L., Zhang, X., & Li, Z. (2016). The WEPP model application in a small watershed in the Loess Plateau. *PloS One*, *11*(3), e0148445.

He, G. (July, 2014). In China's heartland, a toxic trail leads from factories to fields to food. *Yale Environment 360*. Retrieved from http://e360.yale.edu/feature/chinas_toxic_trail_leads_from_factories_to_food/2784/

Huang, X., Li, M. M., Friedli, H. R., Song, Y., Chang, D., & Zhu, L. (2011). Mercury emissions from biomass burning in China. *Environmental Science & Technology*, *45*(21), 9442–9448.

Ju, X. T., Zhang, F. S., Bao, X. M., Römheld, V., & Roelcke, M. (September, 2005). Utilization and management of organic wastes in Chinese agriculture: Past, present and perspectives. *Science in China Series C: Life Sciences*, *48*(2), 965–979.

Kateb, H. E., Zhang, H. F., Zhang, P. C., & Mosandl, R. (2013). Soil erosion and surface runoff on different vegetation covers and slope gradients: A field experiment in Southern Shaanxi Province, China. *Catena*, *105*, 1–10.

Kong, B., & Yu, H. (2013). Estimation model of soil freeze-thaw erosion in Silingco Watershed Wetland of Northern Tibet. *The Scientific World Journal*, *2013*. Article ID 636521, 7 pages.

LADA. (October, 2010). *China National Level Report of Land Degradation Assessment in Drylands*. Prepared by: LADA Project Team, P. R. China. Rome: FAO.

Lee, S. S., Chang, S. X., Chang, Y. Y., & Ok, Y. S. (October, 2013). Commercial versus synthesized polymers for soil erosion control and growth of Chinese cabbage. *SpringerPlus*, *2*(1), 534. Retrieved 15 December 2016 from http://springerplus.springeropen.com/articles/10.1186/2193-1801-2-534

Li, F. R., Kang, L. F., Gao, X. Q., Hua, W., Yang, F. W., & Hei, W. L. (2007). Traffic-related heavy metal accumulation in soils and plants in Northwest China. *Soil & Sediment Contamination*, *16*(5), 473–484. DOI: 10.1080/1532038070149168

Li, Y. X., Yu, Y., Yang, Z. F., Shen, Z. Y., Wang, X., & Cai, Y. P. (2016). A comparison of metal distribution in surface dust and soil among super city, town, and rural area. *Environmental Science and Pollution Research*, *23*(8), 7849–7860. DOI: 10.1007/s11356-015-5911-7

Liu, G. N., Wang, J., Zhang, E., Hou, J., & Liu, X. H. (2016). Heavy metal speciation and risk assessment in dry land and paddy soils near mining areas at Southern China. *Environmental Science and Pollution Research*, *23*(9), 8709–8720. DOI: 10.1007/s11356-016-6114-6

Liu, J. (Ed.). (1996). *Macro-Scale Survey and Dynamic Study of Natural Resources and Environment of China by Remote Sensing*. Beijing: China Science and Technology Publishing House (in Chinese).

Liu, P., Cheng, J., & Liu, X. N. (2015). Soil erosion modulus calculating method. Publication number CN104699962A. Retrieved from www.google.com/patents/CN104699962A?cl=en

Liu, Q. P. (2014). Distribution of fertilizer application and its environmental risk in different provinces of China. *Scientia Agricultura Sinica, 47*(18), 3596–3605. DOI: 10.3864/j.issn.0578–1752.2014.18.008 (in Chinese).

Lu, Y. L., Song, S., Wang, R. S., Liu, Z. Y., Meng, J., Sweetman, A. J., Jenkins, A., Ferrier, R. C., Li, H., Luo, W., & Wang, T. (2015). Impacts of soil and water pollution on food safety and health risks in China. *Environment International, 77*: 5–15. Retrieved 15 December 2016 from http://dx.doi.org/10.1016/j.envint.2014.12.010

MEP. (2003). *Temporary Regulation of Ecological Function Zone* (生态功能区划暂行规程) (in Chinese). Beijing: Ministry of Environmental Protection. Retrieved from http://sts.mep.gov.cn/stbh/stglq/200308/t20030815_90755.shtml

MEP. (2014). *National Soil Pollution Condition Investigation Communique* (土地污染调查公报) (in Chinese). Beijing: Ministry of Environmental Protection. Retrieved 15 December 2016 from www.gov.cn/foot/site1/20140417/782bcb88 840814ba158d01.pdf

NBSC. (2015). *National Bureau of Statistics of China: Statistical Yearbooks 2015.* Beijing: China Statistics Press. Retrieved 15 December 2016 from www.stats.gov. cn/tjsj/ndsj/2015/indexch.htm

Nieuwenhuis, M. (May, 2016). China's Desertification Is Causing Trouble across Asia. Retrieved 15 December 2016 from http://theconversation.com/chinas-desertification-is-causing-trouble-across-asia-59417

OSU. (2016). OSU Spatial Climate Analysis Service. Climate Source. Retrieved 15 December 2016 from www.climatesource.com/cn/fact_sheets/chinappt_xl.jpg

Patton, D. (2015). China farm pollution worsens, despite moves to curb excessive fertilisers, pesticides. *Reuters.* Retrieved 15 December 2016 from http://uk.reuters. com/article/us-china-agriculture-pollution-idUKKBN0N50L720150414

People's Daily. (August, 2000). Farming-pasturing area faces rapid desertification. *People's Daily.* Retrieved 15 December 2016 from http://en.people.cn/english/200008/23/eng20000823_48808.html

Qiu, J. (2010). China faces up to groundwater crisis. *Nature, 466*(7304), 308.

Ran, Y. H., Li, X., Cheng, G. D., Zhang, T. J., Wu, Q. B., Jin, H. J., & Jin, R. (2012). Short communication distribution of permafrost in China: An overview of existing permafrost maps. *Permafrost and Periglacial Processes, 23*(4), 322–333.

Rao, E., Xiao, Y., Ouyang, Z., & Yu, X. (2015). National assessment of soil erosion and its spatial patterns in China. *Ecosystem Health and Sustainability, 1*(4), 1–10. Retrieved from http://dx.doi.org/10.1890/EHS14-0011.1

Roberts, D. (October, 2015). Creating a desert in China: Beijing pressures herders to move to the cities. *Bloomberg.* Retrieved 15 December 2016 from www. bloomberg.com/news/articles/2015-10-01/china-mongolian-desert-herders-under-pressure-to-move-to-cities

Smil, V. (2013). China's environment and natural resources. In: Hudson, C. (Ed.) *The China Handbook,* London: Routledge. Ch. 14.

Steinbock, D. (2010). China's Urbanization: It Has Only Just Begun. New Geography. Retrieved 15 December 2016 from www.newgeography.com/content/001906-china%E2%80%99s-urbanization-it-has-only-just-begun

Sun, B., Zhang, L. X., Yang, L. Z., Zhang, F. S., Norse, D., & Zhu, Z. L. (2012). Agricultural non-point source pollution in China: Causes and mitigation measures. *Ambio, 41*(4), 370–379. DOI: 10.1007/s13280-012-0249-6

Tan, D. (April, 2014). The State of China's Agriculture. China Water Risk. Retrieved from http://chinawaterrisk.org/resources/analysis-reviews/the-state-of-chinas-agriculture/

Tang, J., & Wu, K. (2012). Trend of Acid Rain over China since the 1990s. 2013 NOAA ESRL Global monitoring annual conference. David Skaggs Research Center, Boulder, Colorado, Tuesday 21 May 2013. Retrieved 15 December 2016 from www.esrl.noaa.gov/gmd/publications/annual_meetings/2013/abstracts/30-130408-C.pdf

Tao, W. (2014). Aeolian desertification and its control in Northern China. *International Soil and Water Conservation Research, 2*(4), 34–41.

Tsunekawa, A., Liu, G., Yamanaka, N., & Du, S. (2014). *Restoration and Development of the Degraded Loess Plateau, China.* Heidelberg: Springer.

Wang, M. E., Chen, W. P., & Peng, C. (2016). Risk assessment of Cd polluted paddy soils in the industrial and township areas in Hunan, Southern China. *Chemosphere, 144*, 346–351. Retrieved from http://dx.doi.org/10.1016/j.chemosphere.2015.09.001

Wee, S. L., & Jourdan, A. (2013). In China, public anger over secrecy on environment. *Reuters*. Retrieved 15 December 2015 from www.reuters.com/article/us-china-parliament-pollution-idUSBRE92900R20130310

WLE. (2016). Restoring Pastoral Landscapes in China. Water, Land and Ecosystems. Retrieved from https://wle.cgiar.org/content/restoring-pastoral-landscapes-china

World Bank. (March, 2007). *Restoring China's Loess Plateau*. New York: The World Bank Group. Retrieved from www.worldbank.org/en/news/feature/2007/03/15/restoring-chinas-loess-plateau

World Economic Forum. (December, 2012). What if the world's soil runs out? *Time Magazine*. Retrieved from http://world.time.com/2012/12/14/what-if-the-worlds-soil-runs-out/

WWF. (2014). Ecological Footprint and Sustainable Consumption in China. WWF and China-ASEAN Environmental Cooperation Center. Retrieved from www.footprintnetwork.org/images/article_uploads/China_EF_Sustainable_Consumption_2014_English.pdf

Xinhua. (May, 2011). China to subsidize herdsmen to curb overgrazing. *China Daily*. Retrieved from www.chinadaily.com.cn/china/2011-05/06/content_12459023.htm

Yan, X. D., Gao, D., Zhang, F., Zeng, C., Xiang, W., & Zhang, M. (2013). Relationships between heavy metal concentrations in roadside topsoil and distance to road edge based on field observations in the Qinghai-Tibet Plateau, China. *International Journal of Environmental Research and Public Health, 10*(3), 762–775. DOI: 10.3390/ijerph10030762

Yang, M. X. (September, 2012). The damaging truth about Chinese fertiliser and pesticide use. *China Dialogue*. Retrieved 15 December 2016 from www.china-dialogue.net/article/show/single/en/5153-The-damaging-truth-about-Chinese-fertiliser-and-pesticide-use

Yang, M. X., Wang, S. L., Yao, T. D., Gou, X. H., Lua, A. X., & Guo, X. J. (2004). Desertification and its relationship with permafrost degradation in Qinghai-Xizang (Tibet) plateau. *Cold Regions Science and Technology, 39*(1), 47–53.

68   *Causes of soil degradation and pollution*

Yang, X. Y., & Fang, S. B. (2015). Practices, perceptions, and implications of fertilizer use in East-Central China. *Ambio*, *44*(7), 647–652. DOI: 10.1007/s13280-015-0639-7

Yin, R. S., Xu, J. T., Li, Z., & Liu, C. (2005). China's ecological rehabilitation: The unprecedented efforts and dramatic impacts of reforestation and slope protection in Western China. *China Environment Series*, *6*, 17–32.

Zhang, J. J., Wang, Y., Liu, J. S., Liu, Q., & Zhou, Q. H. (2016). Multivariate and geostatistical analyses of the sources and spatial distribution of heavy metals in agricultural soil in Gongzhuling, Northeast China. *Journal of Soils and Sediments*, *16*(2), 634–644. DOI: 10.1007/s11368-015-1225-0

Zhang, R. F., Wang, X., Fan, H. M., Zhou, L. L., Wu, M., & Liu, Y. H. (2009). Study on the regionalization of freeze-thawing zones in China and the erosion characteristics (in Chinese). *Science of Soil and Water Conservation*, *7*(2), 24–28.

Zhang, W. J., Jiang, F. B., & Ou, J. F. (2011). Global pesticide consumption and pollution: With China as a focus. *Proceedings of the International Academy of Ecology and Environmental Sciences*, *1*(2), 125–144.

Zhang, D., Huang, G., Xu, Y., & Gong, Q. (2015a). Waste-to-Energy in China: Key Challenges and Opportunities. *Energies*, *8*(12), 14182–14196. DOI: 10.3390/en81212422

Zhang, W. T., Zhou, J. Q., Feng, G. L., Weindorf, D. C., Hu, G. Q., & Sheng, J. D. (2015b). Characteristics of water erosion and conservation practice in arid regions of Central Asia: Xinjiang Province, China as an example. *International Soil and Water Conservation Research*, *3*(2), 97–111. Retrieved from http://dx.doi.org/10.1016/j.iswcr.2015.06.002

Zhang, X. Y., Zhong, T. Y., Liu, L., Zhang, X. M., Cheng, M., Li, X. H., & Jin, J. (2016). Chromium occurrences in arable soil and its influence on food production in China. *Environmental Earth Sciences*, *75*(3): 1–8. DOI: 10.1007/s12665-015-5078-z

Zhao, F. J., Ma, Y. B., Zhu, Y. G., Tang, Z., & McGrath, S. P. (2015). Soil contamination in China: Current status and mitigation strategies. American Chemical Society. *Environmental Science & Technology*, *49*(2), 750–759. DOI: 10.1021/es5047099

Zhao, P., Li, L., Wang, L., & Deng, C. (2015). Spatial distributions of national poor counties and soil water erosion in China. *Fresenius Environmental Bulletin*, *24*(12A), 4408–4415. Retrieved from www.researchgate.net/publication/292411333_Spatial_distributions_of_national_poor_counties_and_soil_water_erosion_in_China

Zheng, L., Song, J., Li, C., Gao, Y., Geng, P., Qu, B., & Lin, L. (2014). Preferential policies promote municipal solid waste (MSW) to energy in China: Current status and prospects. *Renewable and Sustainable Energy Reviews*, *36*, 135–148.

Zhou, M., & Zhang, Q. (2003). *The Environmental Problems of Daxinganling Forest in China*. Rome: Food and Agriculture Organization. Retrieved 15 December 2016 from www.fao.org/docrep/ARTICLE/WFC/XII/0959-B3.HTM#P14_153

Zhou, Z., Wu, W., Chen, Q., & Chen, S. (2008). Study on sustainable development of rural household energy in northern China. *Renewable and Sustainable Energy Reviews*, *12*(8), 2227–2239.

4   The impacts of soil degradation and soil pollution

Introduction

Soil degradation and soil pollution have broad impacts. The direct impacts of soil degradation include soil nutrient loss, soil salinization, soil acidification, and desertification. These processes reduce the quality of the soil and its availability for farming. They often occur on marginal soil in the less densely inhabited areas of the north and the west. There is little fertile soil in these regions, so any further degradation of the little fertile land there is has great influence on grain output and livestock production and carries considerable negative consequences for the people. However, perhaps of even greater importance are the indirect impacts, which also affect the densely populated and economically prosperous eastern provinces. Indirect impacts go beyond the site-specific ones directly observable in the field and include dust storms, flooding, landslides, and the siltation of dams, which reduces hydroelectric output. These carry high economic costs and affect the whole country.

Soil pollution directly affects the quality of the food. Food is contaminated by heavy metal, a by-product of poorly standardized industrial activities and the application of excessive amounts of pesticides. Its impact is of great concern to Chinese people, who are aware of the low quality of their food because of regular food poisoning scares. Indeed, China is one of the countries with the highest incidence of food poisoning. The impact of soil pollution is perhaps even more worrisome than soil degradation because it happens in the provinces with the largest agricultural output. It is difficult, time-consuming, and expensive to clean polluted land, and since China already has little land per capita, a reduction of farmland due to its mismanagement is particularly alarming. This chapter first describes the direct and indirect impacts of soil degradation and then the impacts of soil pollution.

The direct impacts of soil degradation

Soil nutrients loss

Soil nutrients are essential for proper crop development. These vital elements can be grouped into three categories; primary (macro) nutrients, secondary nutrients, and micronutrients.

Primary (macro) nutrients that are needed as fertilizers include N (nitrogen), P (phosphorus), and K (potassium). Nitrogen in soil is essential for plant growth, plant cell division, and the formation of amino acids, which are the building blocks of protein. Phosphorus is vital for plant cell division and enlargement, energy transfer and storage, and the respiration and photosynthesis of plants. Potassium is essential for protein synthesis, the breakdown and translocation of starches, plant carbohydrate metabolism, and improving winter hardiness (Barker and Pilbeam, 2015).

Secondary nutrients, sometimes referred to as "synthesizers", are needed in smaller amounts by most crops. These elements are Ca (calcium), Mg (magnesium), and S (sulfur), and their primary function is supporting plant growth and health. Calcium strengthens cell walls, magnesium aids the production of the green pigment in chlorophyll, and sulfur is essential for protein synthesis (Barker and Pilbeam, 2015).

The micronutrients include B (boron), Cl (chlorine), Cu (copper), Fe (iron), Mn (manganese), Mo (molybdenum), and Zn (zinc). These plant nutrients are needed in very small amounts, but since they play an important role as activators of many plant functions, their presence is just as crucial for plant development and crop production as the presence of the major nutrients (Barker and Pilbeam, 2015).

Soils may contain several hundred to several thousand pounds of N, P, or K per acre; however, growing plants can only absorb these nutrients in the forms of available N (AN), available P (AP), and available K (AK). More than half of China's cultivated land lacks microelements, phosphorus, and potassium, and has a soil organic carbon (SOC) content of only 1.8 per cent, much lower than in most European countries. For example, SOC stocks in Chinese soils are only 50 per cent of those found in Finnish, Irish, and Norwegian soils (Li et al., 2016).

Soils throughout the country suffer from secondary nutrient deficiency, especially a lack of Ca and S, and unfortunately areas with secondary nutrient deficiency are constantly growing. In particular, there is a shortage of Mg in the south, scarcity of S in the northeast, Henan, and Inner Mongolia, and deficiency of Ca in southeast China. Furthermore, areas lacking in available Zn and Fe have grown from 51.5 per cent and 5 per cent in 1990s to 65.8 per cent and 24.4 per cent of the total land in 2002, respectively (Chen, 2016).

In addition, SOC is an important component that supports ecological processes and affects the thermal and hydraulic properties as well as the moisture regimes of soil. A loss of SOC results in the reduction of soil fertility, an increase in CO_2 emissions, and land degradation and may even cause desertification (Wei et al., 2015).

Spatially, the highest SOC concentration in the topsoil can be found in the peat and forested areas of the southeastern Tibet mountains and the forest areas in northeast China that are less disturbed by human activities, while the north and northwest, especially in the desert areas, have the lowest values (Wei et al., 2015). Wei et al. (2015) also mapped the spatial distribution of soil nutrients. The distribution of total N and available N show similarities to that of SOC. The Qinghai-Tibet plateau has high total values of P, while the south, the north, and the desert areas are characterized by a low total value of P. The total P contents decrease when the temperature and precipitation of the soil increase. The amount of available K decreases from the north to the south, and total K values are low in tropical areas, while the Qinghai-Tibet Plateau and northeast China are characterized by high total K values (Wei et al., 2015).

Soil nutrient losses are often the result of soil erosion. According to Lu, a researcher at China's Institute of Soil and Water Conservation, "During the heavy rain, the outflow of soil reaches up to one centimeter, resulting in soil fertility decline [as rain washes away fertile soil on the surface layer, exposing poor soil below] inevitably decreasing food production" (Jie, 2010). In agricultural slope land, the eroded sediment is the primary pathway for soil nutrient loss. Hamilton also reported that in the Loess Plateau, 98 per cent of the nutrient loss became sediment in the local rivers (Zhang, 2016). Zhang (2016)'s study explored the influence of rainfall intensity on soil nutrient loss. The results showed that nutrient loss increased exponentially with the increase in rainfall intensity. OM (organic matter), total phosphorous, and total nitrogen losses with a precipitation of 140mm/h were 4, 2.5, and 3 times the value with a precipitation of 60mm/h, respectively. Zhang (2016)'s study also indicated that runoff sediment was the primary pathway for nutrient loss.

Soil salinization

By definition, saline soil contains a high enough concentration of soluble salts to influence plant growth (Li et al., 2016). However, salinity becomes a problem when the high levels of sodium accumulated in the root zone start to interfere with plant growth. Too much salt stresses the plant by preventing the roots from absorbing water from the soil, and excessive amounts of salt in the transpiration stream can damage the cells of the transpiring leaves, further affecting plant growth (McKersie and Lesheim, 2013). This phenomenon is known as the salt-specific or ion-excess effect of salinity (Greenway and Munns, 1980). In its early stages, the dissolved salt content decreases soil productivity by affecting the metabolism of soil organisms, but in the long run it ruins the vegetation and other organisms living in the soil, essentially transforming arable land to infertile, desertified lands (McKersie and Lesheim, 2013).

Soil salinization may be caused by different factors. High soil salinity levels may be attributed to physical or chemical weathering, as well as transport from parent material, geological deposits, or groundwater. The accumulation of salts can also be caused by underlying parent rock constituents, such as carbonate minerals and/or feldspars, or by the one-time submergence of soils under seawater (Salama et al., 1999). Wind and air may also cause the accumulation of salts in coastal zones. The inland wind can carry the salt from the sea over long distances as spindrift, or the salt can fall to the ground with the rainwater after being carried by the warm northwesterly winds. According to Yang (2006), climate change is another significant driving factor in the salinization of the soil. North and northeast China in particular are becoming warmer and drier, which contributes to the increasing salinization of the region's soils.

The salinized land is mainly distributed in areas with a higher groundwater table and higher evaporation. In arid areas, saline soils may be formed through evaporation and the lack of rainfall to flush the soils. Waterlogging may also cause salinization: in semi-arid regions where waterlogging is followed by drought, when rain falls, the water dissolves the salt naturally found in the soil and brings it to the surface. When the water evaporates, the salt remains on the surface (Mao et al., 2002). In addition, the water used for irrigation (whether river or groundwater) also contains salts, which remain behind in the soil after the water has evaporated. Furthermore, impeded drainage in areas irrigated by continuous flooding (as is the case with paddy rice) causes secondary salinization (LADA, 2010). In the oasis basin of Xinjiang in northwest China, the area of salinized soil makes up about 1.05 million ha, which accounts for 33.4 per cent of the total agricultural land in the region, and research has found that the salinity of this area is trending upwards.

According to Zhang et al. (2014), the area of salinized soil in China is about 36.93 million ha, which accounts for about one-third of the total arable land. Studies showed that when the concentration of salt ions in the soil exceeds 8 g per kg of soil, it can severely damage or prevent crop growth on farmlands (Zhang et al., 2014). Table 4.1 shows the salt tolerance of crops in China's different regions.

Table 4.1 Salt tolerance of crops in the different regions of China

Region	Soil depth	Salinity (per cent)			
		Lightly inhibiting growth	*Moderately inhibiting growth*	*Severely inhibiting growth*	*Preventing growth*
Northeast	0–50 cm (SO_4^{2-})	0.3–0.5	0.5–0.7	0.7–1.2	
Shandong Province	surface soil layer (total salt content)	< 0.2	0.2–0.4	0.4–0.8	
	100 cm (total salt content)	< 0.1	0.1–0.3	0.3–0.5	
North China	0–20 cm (CL-SO_4^{2-})	0.15–0.25	0.25–0.40	0.40–0.60	
Northwest	0–30 cm (SO_4^{2-})	0.4–0.8	0.8–1.2	1.2–2.0	> 2.0
	0–100 cm (SO_4^{2-})	0.3–0.6	0.6–1.0	1.0–1.5	> 1.5
Xinjiang Province	0–30 cm (total salt content)	0.554–0.727	0.727–0.866	0.866–1.345	> 1.345
	0–100 cm (total salt content)	0.391–0.491	0.491–0.597	0.597–0.895	> 0.895

Source: MEP (2003), Table B3

Soil acidification

Soil pH is a critical measure for plant growth. Crops generally thrive in slightly acidic (with a pH value lower than 7) or neutral (with a pH value of 7) soils. When the pH value decreases, the soil becomes susceptible to diseases and pests that slow down plant growth. Heavily acidic conditions also cause toxic metals to leak into nearby bodies of water. Moreover, soil acidification can help to increase the accumulation of some heavy metals like Cd in food crops (Hvistendahl, 2010).

During the early 1980s, a national soil survey determined the pH values of topsoils. To understand the changes in soil acidity that have occurred between the 1980s and the 2000s, Guo et al. (2010)

> collected all published data on topsoil pH from 2000 to 2008 and compiled two (unpaired) data sets (1980s versus 2000s) on the basis of six soil groups according to geography and use, with two subgroups per soil group: cereal crops and cash crops.
>
> (Guo et al., 2010: 1008)

Both cropping systems – especially cash crops like greenhouse vegetables that have spread rapidly since the 1980s – received very high fertilizer inputs compared to other agricultural systems (Guo et al., 2010). The results showed a considerable acidification of all topsoils, with an average pH decline of 0.13 to 0.8. In all other soil groups, acidification has been more significant in cash crops (pH decreased by 0.3 to 0.8) than cereals (a drop of 0.13 to 0.76). In some areas, the pH values dropped by 0.8 over two decades, with some soils growing high-input cash crops reaching a pH of 5.07. As a comparison, when soil is left under natural conditions, it takes at least 100 years to reach this level of acidification (Gilbert, 2010). As the scale is logarithmic, a pH decrease of 0.3 corresponds to a doubling in hydrogen ion activity (Guo et al., 2010). Acidification has already decreased crop production by 30–50 per cent in some areas.

Zhang Fusuo, a professor of plant nutrition at China Agricultural University in Beijing, said that "in the south, the heavy use of fertilizers has pushed the pH to 3 or 4 in some places. Maize, tobacco, and tea cannot be grown. This is a long-term effect". He claimed that if the degradation of soil continues, some regions could see the soil pH drop to as low as 3 in the long run, and warned that "no crop can grow at this level of acidification" (in Tan, 2010).

Hou et al. (2012)'s study in Foshan (Guangdong Province) showed that 90 per cent of the soil samples in the study area had a pH < 4.5, and only 8 per cent of soils had a pH within the range 4.5–5.5 in the year 2008 and 2009. This can be compared to 80 per cent of the soil samples that were in that range during 1979–1984 (Figure 4.1).

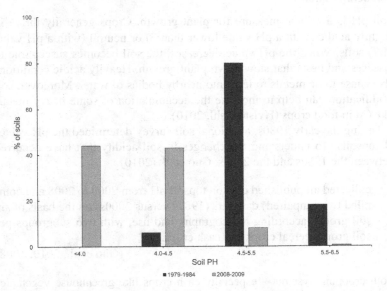

Figure 4.1 Comparison of pH of natural soils in Foshan (Guangdong Province) during 1979–1984 and 2008–2009

Source: Hou et al. (2012)

Desertification

According to Yongli Zhang, deputy head of the State Forestry Administration, "land desertification poses the most serious threat to ecological development in China". According to Zhang, China now has 261 million ha of soil that is classified as undergoing desertification. This corresponds to about 27.2 per cent of the country's mainland and is spread across 528 counties in 18 provinces, autonomous regions, and municipalities, directly affecting some 400 million people (Hao, 2016).

The process of desertification is due to various factors, both natural and man-made. Natural causes include wind erosion, water erosion, and freeze-thawing erosion, which in China have caused the desertification of 183.2 million ha, 25.52 million ha, and 36.35 million ha of land, respectively (Figure 4.2). Desertification is mostly observed in the provincial

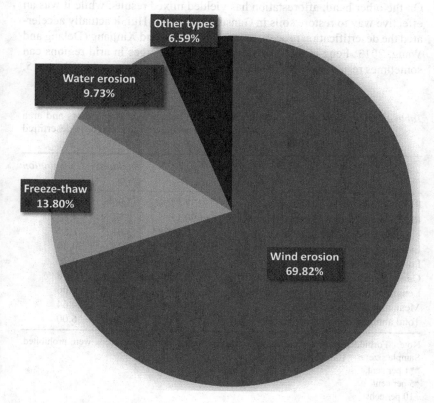

Figure 4.2 Distribution of different desertification types
Source: SFA (2011)

regions of Xinjiang, Inner Mongolia, Tibet, Gansu, and Qinghai, which together account for 95.48 per cent of the total area of desertified lands in China (SFA, 2011).

Feng et al. (2015) looked at the natural and man-made causes of desertification. Using a pooled regression model based on panel data, Feng et al. (2015) assessed the effects of climate change and human activities on the desertified areas of Xinjiang, Inner Mongolia, Gansu, and Ningxia Hui between 1983 and 2012. The results showed that "livestock number, farmland area, road construction, and mean annual temperature were significantly positively related to the change in the area of desertification, accounting for 30.8, 21.9, 4.1, and 14.6 per cent of the total effect, respectively" (Feng et al., 2015: 4) (Table 4.2). The findings (Figure 4.3) also revealed that the most dominant driving factors varied across the regions, and so did the solutions. Livestock contributed to desertification in all regions, suggesting that forbidding grazing would be an effective approach to ecological restoration. On the other hand, afforestation has yielded mixed results: while it was an effective way to restore soils in Gansu and Ningxia Hui, it actually accelerated the desertification process in Inner Mongolia and Xinjiang (Delang and Wang, 2013; Feng et al., 2015). Indeed, planting trees in arid regions can sometimes result in greater desertification, as will be discussed in Chapter 5.

Table 4.2 Regression results for the relationship between driving factors and area of desertification, and contribution of each factor to changes in desertified areas (1990–2010)

	Pooled	*Standard error*	*Contribution (%)*
Rural population ($\times 10^9$ persons)	−177.5**	−3.90	10.55
Rural net income ($\times 10^6$ RMB)	−690.1*	−2.74	7.80
Farmland area ($\times 10^6$ ha)	0.987**	−3.61	21.87
Livestock number ($\times 10^9$ head)	11.050**	−7.24	30.80
Forbidden area ($\times 10^6$ ha)	−1.177*	−2.89	4.20
Cumulative afforestation area ($\times 10^6$ ha)	−0.00792	−0.09	0.08
Length of roads and railways ($\times 10^6$ km)	16.90*	−3.05	4.06
Mean annual temperature (°C)	39.20+	−2.14	14.64
Total annual precipitation (mm)	−5.898+	−2.33	6.00

Note: "Forbidden area" represents areas where grazing and growing crops were prohibited. Sample size: $n = 108$. Significance levels:
**1 per cent,
*5 per cent,
+10 per cent.

Source: Feng et al. (2015)

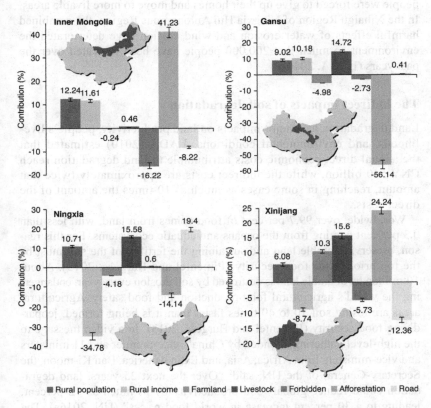

Figure 4.3 Contribution rates (per cent) of the factors affecting desertified areas based on regression analysis results

Note: "Road" represents the length of roads and railways.

Source: Feng et al. (2015)

Sandification has been a source of various problems to the farmers and herdsmen, eventually leading to the impoverishment of the local population and the vicious cycle of people exploiting the environment unsustainably to try to maintain their already poor standards of living, which further degrades the environment. LADA (2010) reports how in the northern part of the Yinshan Mountains of Inner Mongolia, wind erosion and sandification significantly hinder agricultural output and animal husbandry, as well as the everyday life of local people. As a result, the Yinshan Mountains are home to 23.4 per cent of the poorest people of Inner Mongolia. In the Chayouhou Banner and Huade County of Inner Mongolia, over 90,000 people were forced to give up their homes and move to more livable areas. In the Xihaigu Region of Ningxia Hui Autonomous Region, the combined harmful effects of water erosion and wind erosion have deteriorated the environment so much that 200,000 people have been relocated over the past years (LADA, 2010).

The indirect impacts of soil degradation

Land degradation has major impacts on land productivity, people's livelihoods, and environmental conditions. LADA (2010) estimated that the annual direct economic costs attributable to land degradation reach CNY 540 billion, while the indirect costs are approximately twice that amount, reaching in some cases as much as 10 times the amount of the direct costs.

Worldwide, over 99.7 per cent of food comes from land, with less than 0.3 per cent coming from the oceans and aquatic ecosystems. For this reason, preserving arable land and sustaining the fertility of the soil must be the top priority for food security (Pimentel and Burgess, 2013). About 10 million ha of arable land is destroyed by soil erosion every year, endangering the world's agricultural food production and food safety. Agricultural areas are losing soil 10 to 40 times faster than it is being formed, jeopardizing food security (Pimentel and Burgess, 2013). In a video message to the high-level gathering attended by China's vice-premier and 11 ministers and vice-ministers from Africa, Asia, and Latin America, Ban Ki-moon, the Secretary-General of the UN, said: "Over the next 25 years, land degradation could reduce global food productivity by as much as 12 percent, leading to a 30 percent increase in world food prices" (UN, 2016a). The problem is exacerbated by the fact that two-thirds of the world's population is already malnourished, according to the World Health Organization and the Food and Agricultural Organization. Ban Ki-moon warned: "Without a long-term solution, desertification and land degradation will not only affect food supply, but lead to increased migration and threaten the stability of many nations and regions" (UN, 2016a).

Impact of land degradation on production processes

With over 40 per cent of its land area being affected by erosion, China is subjected to the world's most severe soil degradation. One direct consequence of land degradation is the reduction of land usable for agriculture and the decrease of land productivity, because the loss of surface soil layers with rich organic matter and nutrients will decrease the fertility and moisture-holding capability of the soil. In addition, secondary salinization of the soil leads to soil hardening, which results in a decline in productivity (LADA, 2010). The main problems are as follows:

Reduction in grain output

Although there has been a significant improvement in cereal yields over the last few years (Figure 4.4), it is uncertain whether this upward trend will continue (Wei et al., 2015). According to an official report released in 2016, China could experience a drop in wheat production for the first time in 12 years (Xu, 2016). Li et al. (2013) argued that the future food security of China is challenged by problems such as soil degradation and

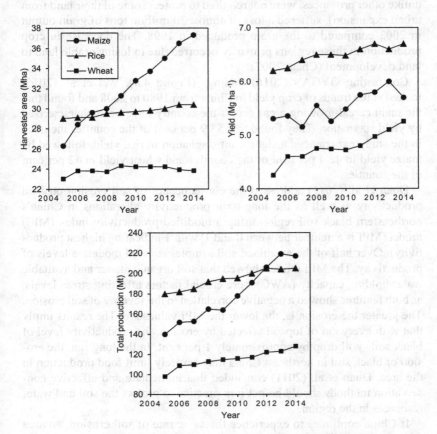

Figure 4.4 (A) Harvested areas, (B) average yield, and (C) total production of rice, maize, and wheat in China (2005–2014)

Source: GYGA (2016)

pollution, the low efficiency of resource use, and the competition for non-agricultural land uses. Indeed, in addition to the degradation of the soil, some of the most fertile agricultural land is being converted to urban uses (e.g. parks, roads, housing, and industrial complexes). Chen (2007) argued that urbanization has led to the irreparable damage of the physical and biotic characteristics of the soil, resulting in the total loss of productivity: in the event of a grain supply emergency, quick reconversion of urban land to crop production would not be possible. The same study also found that urbanization progressed much quicker in heavily populated areas where soils had previously not suffered serious degradation. For instance, the coastal provinces of Jiangsu and Guangdong in southeast China (which, unlike other provinces, were not required to protect some of their land from urban expansion), suffered a loss of almost 30 million tons of grain output in 2003 compared to the grain produced in 1998. The decrease in crop production in these regions primarily occurred due to losing arable land to land development (Chen, 2007).

Contrasting GYGA's (2016) findings (Figure 4.4), Wei et al. (2015) looked at the trends of crop yield in China from 1980 to 2008 and found that the main cereal-growing areas across the country have been characterized by yield stagnation. They found that 53.9 per cent of the counties included in the study experienced a significant stagnation in rice yield, followed by maize yield in 42.4 per cent of the counties and wheat yield in 42 per cent of the counties.

Duan et al. (2011) addressed the consequences of soil erosion on land productivity as well as the long-term productivity alterations in China's northeastern black soil region using a modified productivity index (MPI) model (MPI is a number between 0 and 1, with 1 indicating highest productivity). Over half of the examined soil samples showed moderate levels of productivity. The MPI model showed that soil organic matter and available water-holding capacity (AWC) were crucial factors affecting stress levels, as both features showed a negative correlation to the severity of soil erosion. The greater the erosion is, the lower the MPI values are. The results imply that with every cm of topsoil affected by erosion, the productivity level of black soils will drop by approximately 1 per cent. In the long run, the erosion of black soil in northeast China may severely limit food production in the area. Duan et al. (2011) concluded that immediate and effective conservation methods should be put into practice to protect the soil and water resources in the region.

If China continues to experience the same rate of soil erosion, an area as large as the islands of Cyprus or Puerto Rico will disappear over the next 50 years – resulting in a 40 per cent drop in food production, according to a study conducted by the country's Ministry of Water Resources and the academies of science and engineering (Ding, 2010). In the same vein, Huang Hongxiang, a researcher from the Institute of Agricultural Resources and Regional Planning, cautioned that China's present focus on production volumes could have a severe impact on its agricultural development:

> If we don't improve the quality of farmland, but only depend on increasing investment and improving technology, then – regardless of whatever super rice, super wheat and other super quality crops we come up with – it will be difficult to guarantee the sustainable development of our nation's agriculture.

(Watts, 2012)

Damages to grassland with reduced livestock products

Grassland degradation is a process in which the vegetation becomes sparser and shorter, with a lower grass density. Grassland productivity is graded based on the dry matter yield of grassland per hectare per year:

(1) high yield: > 2000 kg of dry matter per ha per year;
(2) fair yield: 1000–2000 of kg dry matter per ha per year;
(3) low yield: < 1000 of kg dry matter per ha per year.

Unfortunately, most grasslands in China produce a low yield. In the late 1990s, low-yield areas accounted for two-thirds of the total, while high-yield areas accounted for just over 10 percent of all grasslands (Chen and Fischer, 1998). Figure 4.5 shows the geographic distribution of different yield grades in the late 1990s. Unfortunately, the situation has been worsening since then. The case of the Guyuan pastureland in the northwest Hebei Province (on the Bashang Plateau) may be indicative of many other areas in China. In the 1950s, the hay production of the Guyuan pastureland totaled 250–300 kg per year, with a grazing grass coverage of 90 per cent and grass height of 50–100 cm. Figure 4.5 describes the area as having a fair yield in the late 1990s. By the late 2000s, however, the grass coverage was only about 40 per cent and the grass height 20–40 cm, while the production of hay had decreased to 50–100 kg per annum (LADA, 2010). From a high-yield area in the 1950s, the Guyuan pastureland had become a low-yield area by the late 2000s.

A regional scale survey found that, consistent with land degradation processes, the total C and N content and effective cation exchange capacity (ECEC) of the soil also decreased significantly. Consequently, the productivity of grassland had decreased. In cases of severe soil degradation, it may

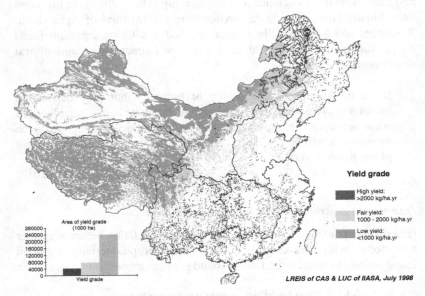

Figure 4.5 Distribution of yield grades of grasslands in China

Source: Chen and Fisher (1998)

be impossible to re-establish the right balance of nutrient stocks in soils (Wu et al., 2008).

Lands under heavy grazing pressure may lose their fertility, which in turn increases the soil's susceptibility to wind erosion, eventually turning the area into a desert. Due to the poorer grassland quality caused by soil degradation, herdsmen can only keep hardier livestock breeds such as goats and camels. With the heavy impact of land degradation, the quality of livestock has also decreased. Herders have tried to increase the number of livestock to compensate for their smaller size, which, ironically, resulted in the per head grazing land areas to drop by 50 per cent, leaving livestock in a semi-hungry state for long periods. The result was a drop in the output of livestock and livestock products. For example, in Uxin Banner in Inner Mongolia, the average weight of sheep dropped from 25 kg in 1950s to 15 kg by the early 2000s, while the weight of goats dropped from 15 kg to 9 kg over the same period (LADA, 2010).

Similar processes happened to cultivated fields. Lu and Chen (2013) claimed that there was a link between the poor agricultural land and people's poverty in the western counties: poor farmers could not afford to expand production on their existing land because of the low productive capacity of the land, the poor agricultural infrastructure, and insufficient capital accumulation. Under these conditions, farmers had no choice but to expand their land to increase agricultural output and incomes by turning woodlands, grasslands, and steep lands into farmlands, regardless of these lands' suitability for agriculture. However, the gradual degradation of the quality of the land, together with the expansion of the population, results in a vicious circle which makes it increasingly difficult to raise incomes and use the environment sustainably. Eventually, soil erosion consigned the area into a long-term poverty trap (Lu and Chen, 2013). According to LADA (2010), although the north and the west have a population density of only 43 per cent – and 1.76 times as much land – as the eastern areas, the per capita grain production in the north and the west is only 50 per cent of that in the east, their per capita consumption and savings are only 33 per cent, the density of schools is only 49 per cent, and that of clinics is only 8 per cent as high, while the quality of these schools and clinics is poorer (LADA, 2010).

Impacts on ecosystem services

Damage to biodiversity

Land degradation has led to the reduction of usable grasslands and forest lands and, through the loss, fragmentation, and isolation of natural habitats, to a reduced level of biodiversity. In addition, it has changed the structure of animal populations and communities, reducing the productivity and liveliness of species (through lower birth/survival rates and pest/disease resistance capability, among others), gradually pushing them to the verge of extinction. For example, in Mu Us Sandy Land (in Central China), many animal and plant species have disappeared or suffered a decline in species distribution or population. For instance, there were more than 5 million Mongolian gazelles (*Procapra gutturosa*) living on the grasslands of Inner Mongolia in the 1950s, but their residual population is now less than 300,000; the leopard, wild cattle, and wild camel have almost become extinct; and the populations of the gray marmot, fox, and wolf have dropped significantly. Land degradation has also caused the extinction of numerous species (LADA, 2010).

Soil degradation, whether caused by drought, salinization, or its over-exploitation, affects the ability of the soil to sustain and regenerate itself (UNESCO, 2003). If a pasture becomes severely degraded, the distribution of various plant species will change. In particular, there will be a reduction in the proportion of palatable plant species such as grasses and grass-like plants. Animals whose food supply depends on this vegetation are forced to migrate to other grazing areas. At the same time, many of these animal species are also valuable resources for the population, and their disappearance may increase food insecurity and threaten people's livelihoods (Wu et al., 2008).

Dust and sandstorms resulting from land degradation

Due to "overgrazing by livestock, overcultivation, excessive water use, or changes in climate" (Economy, 2011: 66), more than a quarter of the total land area of China has been affected by land degradation or desertification. The State Forestry Administration in China stated that the desertification of land is the country's most critical ecological issue, and one that will only be worsened by climate change.

Dust events in China are associated with two main source areas. The first affected region is the Hexi Corridor and the western Inner Mongolia Plateau, which are covered by the Gobi Desert, wadis, and alluvial fans. Stretching across China and Mongolia, the Gobi Desert is the second largest dust source in the world (and the most important one in China) and eats up 360,000 ha of fertile grassland each year. The second largest dust source is the western Taklimakan Desert, followed by the central area of the Inner Mongolia Plateau and northeastern China (Wang, 2014). Experts attribute Beijing's dusty weather to the desertification of vast areas of grazing lands and plains north of the capital in the Autonomous Region of Inner Mongolia, Hebei, and Shanxi provinces. The soil in these dry areas contains a high proportion of sand, and strong winds can transport these sand particles for 3,000 km or even further. The deserts of Gansu Province and Xinjiang Uygur Autonomous Region, which are thousands of miles away, may also be the source of dust storms in Beijing (Pan and Liu, 2011).

Sandstorms are frequent in northern China (Figure 4.6), especially in Inner Mongolia, which experiences some 20 days of sandstorms a year, particularly during the spring. However, they have an impact well beyond the drylands. For example, on 5 May 1993, a catastrophic dust and sandstorm affected 12 million people in 72 counties across four provinces. In total, a 40 million ha area was affected, with casualties of 100 people and thousands of livestock (Liu and Diamond, 2005).

The continuity of drought in winter and spring as well as the damages to ground vegetation has led to the growing deterioration of the environment. However, dust storms not only damage the quality of the environment, they also have negative impacts on health. Many studies have shown a significant correlation between dust events and respiratory and cardiovascular hospitalizations after adjusting for the effects of SO_2 and/or NO_2 exposure (Pan and Liu, 2011). Furthermore, scientists have found that dust clouds

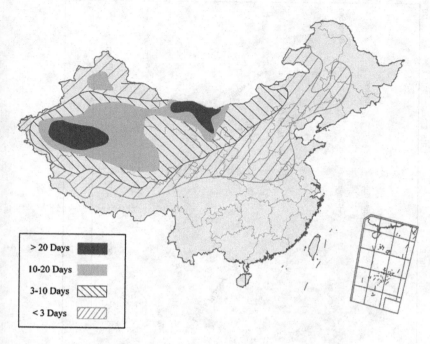

Figure 4.6 Number of days of sandstorms per year
Source: Lorenz et al. (2016)

were possible transmitters of influenza, SARS, and hand, foot, and mouth disease (HFMD), among others (Vidal, 2009).

Floods and landslides

The Yellow River, known as the Huang He in China, supplies water to 155 million people (about 12 per cent of China's population) and irrigates 7.3 million ha (about 15 per cent of China's farmland). More than 400 million people live in the Yellow River basin, and the river is vital for the sustenance of so many people (Wang et al., 2015).

The Yellow River (Figure 4.7) is slow and sluggish along most of its course. Yet it is also one of the wildest and most destructive rivers in the world. Since historians began keeping records in 602 B.C., the river has changed its course 26 times and produced 1,500 floods that have killed millions of people. The root of these disasters is the large amount of silt generated by soil erosion. The Yellow River discharges three times the amount

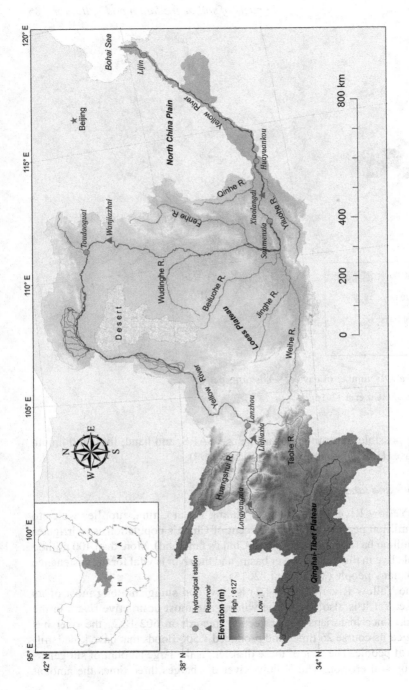

Figure 4.7 Topography of the Yellow River basin

Source: Ran et al. (2013)

of sediment of the Mississippi River, and some regard it as the world's muddiest major river. 1.5 billion tons of silt is washed into the Yellow River every year, and the vast amount of sediment sometimes makes the water look like chocolate milk. Three quarters of this sediment is carried down to the Yellow Sea, and the rest is deposited in the river beds, causing the water level to rise (Wang et al., 2015). According to Mofcom (2009), the silt deposited on the riverbed makes it rise on average 10 cm each year. The result is that the riverbed of many downstream sections of the river is 3 to 5 meters higher than the surrounding land. The "hanging-riverway" situation can result in flooding disasters if the dikes breach (Liu et al., 2014; Luo et al., 1997). As a consequence, soil erosion causes an increase in flooding, not only because the vegetation that once captured rainwater and slowed its flow into the rivers is gone but also because of the rise of the riverbed (Wang et al., 2015).

The water running off the hillsides also intensifies peak river flows, resulting in the erosion of riverbanks and increasing the risk of natural landslides (Figure 4.8). In addition, the more soil is washed into the river, the

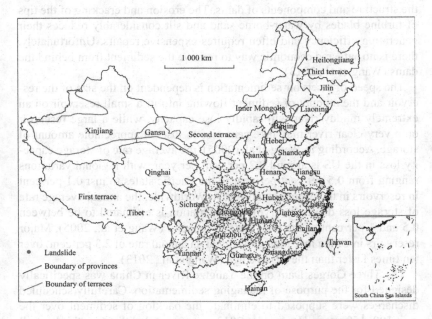

Figure 4.8 Distribution of catastrophic landslides in China since the 20th century

Source: Huang and Li (2011)

less of it remains on the land for farmers to use (Ford, 2011). According to Huang and Li (2011), rainfall and earthquakes are the primary trigger factors of landslides. However, human activities including construction, tree cutting, and farming also contribute to the instability of mountain slopes, which has become the primary cause for the catastrophic landslides that occur in China.

Silt filling in dams

China has built more than half of the large reservoirs in the world since 1950, mainly for the production of hydroelectricity (Gao, Jia et al., 2015). When the silt contained in the rivers reaches the reservoir, it sinks and settles behind the dam. The more sediment a river carries, the faster the silt will accumulate. As the sediment builds up at the bottom of the reservoir, the dam slowly loses its water storage capacity and its original functions, in particular its capacity to generate electricity (Wang et al., 2013).

Besides filling the reservoirs, the large amounts of sediment also damage the structure and components of dams. The erosion and cracking of the tips of turbine blades by water-borne sand and silt considerably reduces their generating efficiency and often requires expensive repairs. Unfortunately, there is no safe and economic way to remove the sediment from behind the dams (Wang et al., 2013).

The speed of reservoir sedimentation is dependent on the size of the reservoir and the amount of sediment flowing into it: a small reservoir on an extremely muddy river will rapidly lose capacity, while a large reservoir on a very clear river may take centuries to lose an appreciable amount of storage. According to Wang et al. (2005), the average rate of storage capacity loss in the US is around 0.2 per cent per year, with regional variations ranging from 0.5 per cent per year in the Pacific states to just 0.1 per cent in reservoirs in the American northeast. Worldwide, the annual average rate of storage loss due to reservoir sedimentation is estimated to be between 0.5 and 1 per cent of the total storage capacity (Wang et al., 2005). Major reservoirs in China lose their capacity at an annual rate of 2.3 per cent, over ten times faster than the US average (Wang et al., 2013).

The Three Gorges Dam on the Yangtze River in China was specifically designed for the purpose of managing sedimentation. Carefully scheduled discharges were supposed to eliminate the backlog of sediment over the next 100–150 years. However, a 2013 report revealed that two-thirds of all river sediments are still blocked behind the dam every year (Wang et al., 2013). Engineers of the Three Gorges Dam predict that by the 2020s, the sedimentation of the Yangtze River could start causing problems upstream in the city of Chongqing. Fan Xiao, a Sichuan Province geologist and a critic of the Three Gorges Project, along with other scientists, claim that due to the rate of sediment accumulation, Chongqing could experience flooding and shipping issues much sooner than that (Yardley, 2007).

According to LADA (2010: 53), since 1981, 29 small-sized reservoirs in Yulin and Yan'an of northern Shaanxi Province, with a total capacity of 62 million m³, have been completely filled up by silt. There are many more examples of reservoirs that have lost at least some of their holding capacity due to siltation (LADA, 2010):

- The Sanmenxia Reservoir in the Yellow River basin was completed in 1960, and by October 1964 it had accumulated 3,750 million m³ of sediment deposits, corresponding to a 62.9 per cent loss of the storage capacity.
- The Shenmuwaluo Reservoir, built in 1977, with a storage capacity of 6.26 million m³, was fully silted up by 1988.
- The Liujiaxia reservoir, built in 1968, accumulated 1.2 billion m³ of silt by 1991.

Table 4.3 shows the sedimentation in the major reservoirs on the Yellow River basin from the 1960s onward to 2000. In total, 13.42 Gt of sediment

Table 4.3 Sedimentation of major reservoirs in the Yellow River basin

Reservoir name	Initial storage capacity (km³)	Filled sediment (Gt)	Time period
Sanmenxia	9.75	8.908	1960–1997
Liujiaxia	5.7	1.833	1968–2000
Longyangxia	24.7	0.277	1986–2000
Qingtongxia	0.62	0.736	1967–2000
Yanguoxia	0.22	0.24	1962–2000
Tianqiao	0.068	0.076	1977–2000
Wangyao	0.203	0.134	1978–2000
Wanjiazhai	0.898	0.078	1997–2000
Bapanxia	0.049	0.038	1970–2000
Bajiazhui	0.525	0.42	1961–2000
Fengjiashan	0.389	0.11	1974–2000
Fenhe	0.7	0.472	1961–2000
Sanshenggong	0.08	0.056	1960–2000
Taoqupo	0.057	0.019	1979–1995
Yangmaowan	0.12	0.023	1973–1995
Total	44.08	13.42	

Source: Ran et al. (2013)

had been trapped in the 15 reservoirs of the Yellow River basin by 2000. For the 601 reservoirs with a storage capacity over 1 million m^3 in the Yellow River basin, the amount of deposited sediment in the backwater zones was estimated at 10.9 billion m^3 in 1989, which accounted for 21 per cent of the total storage capacity at the time (Ran et al., 2013).

Dams can be equipped to flush out the silt. One dam with such facilities is the Xiaolangdi Dam, China's second largest dam facility after the Three Gorges Dam. The dam is used to control flood, reduce silt, produce electricity, and facilitate irrigation, among others (LADA, 2010). The Loess Plateau deposits 1.6 billion tons of silt into the Yellow River annually, and one of the primary functions of the earthen dam is to prevent the river from rising, by storing the silt. During the rainy season, the reservoir holds the water, acting as a buffer against floods. During the dry season, the water is used for irrigation. In addition, during the dry season, the accumulated silt is flushed out through three specialized holes (Xia et al., 2016). As much as 30 million tons of silt is let out every year from the dam's reservoir. The operation lowers the riverbed in the lower reach of the river by an average of 2 meters (Wang et al., 2015). However, the reservoir of the Xiaolangdi Dam has the capacity to store water only until 2020. At that point, it will no longer be possible to release the water and flush out the sediment from the reservoir, and the river levels will once again start to rise. As reported by Xia et al. (2016), according to a dam engineer, "Our children and grandchildren will need to think of another solution to the silt problem."

The impacts of soil pollution

Soil pollution is a serious problem in China. According to Wang Shiyuan, the vice minister of Land and Resources, about 3.33 million ha of China's farmland, an area roughly equal to the size of Belgium, was too degraded for crop production (Wang, 2014). On the other hand, a report published in 2016 by the Ministry of Environmental Protection stated that approximately 17 per cent of China's arable land (nearly 20 million ha) was affected by soil contamination. The report also revealed that each year over 13 million tons of harvested crops were polluted with heavy metals, and 8.9 million ha of arable land were contaminated with pesticides (Wang, 2014). Soil pollution has even more devastating impacts on food production and security than soil degradation and poses major threats to both the ecosystem and the health of the population (Wang, 2014). China's poor food safety levels also led to a rise in food imports from other countries. According to the OECD, in 2001, the country obtained 6.2 per cent of its food through imports, and by 2012 that figure went up to 12.9 per cent (Zhang et al., 2015).

Heavy metal contamination of food

Of all types of pollutants found in China, heavy metal contamination is considered to pose the highest risk to food safety (Lu et al., 2015). The national food safety standard (GB2762–2012) determines the maximum levels of contamination that is allowed in foods. Food contaminants considered in the safety standard include lead (Pb), cadmium (Cd), mercury (Hg), arsenic (As), tin (Sn), nickel (Ni), chromium (Cr), nitrite, benzo[a] pyrene, N-nitrosodimethylamine, polychlorinated biphenyl, 3-chloro-1, 2-propanediol (Clever and Ma, 2014). The human body needs Cu, Zn, and Ni in trace amounts. However, excessive exposure to these metals is damaging to human health.

The presence of heavy metals harmful to the body understandably raises worries due to their environmental persistence. The major routes toxic materials can enter the body are through ingestion with food, inhalation, and absorption through contact with the skin, eyes, or mouth. However, diet dominates the pathways of heavy metal absorption by humans (Su et al., 2014). When crops and vegetables are grown in polluted soils, the pollutants are absorbed by the root system and transferred to the rest of the plant. When the chemicals are ingested, their accumulation in the body can cause a wide range of illnesses. Depending on the type of contaminant, its origin and concentration, the associated/related conditions may range from neurological disorders to osteoporosis and cancer (Li et al., 2014; UBC International Reporting Program, 2016; Warrence et al., 2003).

Research found a connection between exposure to cadmium and kidney cancer (Su et al., 2014). In addition, high Cd levels in the body decrease the uptake of calcium, causing calcium deficiency that may lead to cartilage disorders and bone fractures, among others. Skeletal damage related to long-term cadmium exposure was first reported in Japan, where the itai-itai (ouch-ouch) disease, a combination of osteomalacia and osteoporosis, started around 1912 as a result of a mass Cd poisoning (Lars, 2003).

Lead (Pb) enters the human body through respiration and digestion. Pb may permanently damage many of the body organs, such as the kidney and the liver, as well as the reproductive, nervous, urinary, and immune systems, and the basic physiological processes of cells and gene expression (Su et al., 2014).

Arsenic (As) has been identified as a human carcinogen by the International Agency for Research on Cancer in 1980. The majority of people are constantly exposed to low levels of As. However, high levels of As have been recognized as a cause of lung, bladder, skin, and kidney cancer in humans (Zhou et al., 2016).

Heavy metals do not decompose or degrade like organic pollutants. Instead, they accumulate and transform, posing a long-term toxic threat to

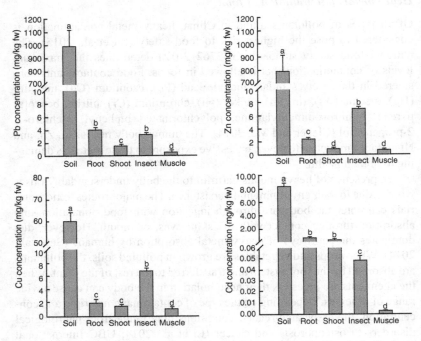

Figure 4.9 Concentrations of Pb, Zn, Cu, and Cd across the food cycle (soil-plant-insect-chicken)

Source: Zhuang et al. (2009)

both human beings and animals. Zhuang et al. (2009) conducted a study about the accumulation and transfer of Pb, Zn, Cu, and Cd across the soil-plant-insect-chicken food chain at contaminated sites (Figure 4.9). The soil had the highest concentration of heavy metals. For some heavy metals (Pb and Cd), plants had a higher concentration than the insects that ate these plants, but for other heavy metals (Zn and Cu), the insects had a higher concentration than plants. Chicken muscle was found to have a lower concentration of heavy metals. In general, the concentrations of heavy metals in the chicken tissues and feces were in the sequence of: feces > liver > muscle > blood. The elimination of Pb, Zn, Cu, and Cd via excretion prevented the bioaccumulation of these metals in the body of chickens. Nevertheless, the concentration of heavy metals in the liver of chickens fed with contaminated insects (3.62 mg/kg fw) was much higher than that in chickens fed with heavy metals-free insects. Zhuang et al. (2009) concluded that "the potential health risk associated with Pb through the consumption of the muscle and liver of chickens could not be neglected" (p. 851).

Acidic soil can increase the risk of transfer of heavy metals from the soil to the food chain. For the rice commonly grown in southern China (*Indica* rice), when soil has a pH of 7, a soil cadmium (Cd) concentration of 0.5 mg kg⁻¹ results in a grain Cd concentration of 0.2 mg kg⁻¹. On the other hand, when soil has a pH of 5, the same soil Cd concentration of 0.5 mg kg⁻¹ results in a grain Cd concentration of 0.45 mg kg⁻¹ (Figure 4.10) (Zhao et al., 2014).

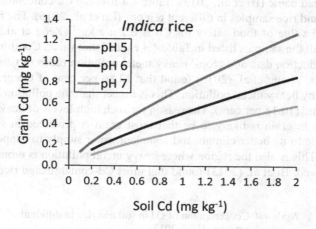

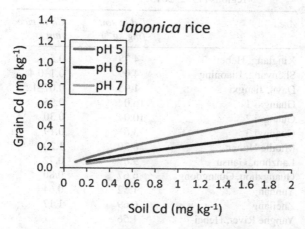

Figure 4.10 Grain Cd concentration in Indica and Japonica rice as a function of soil pH and total soil Cd concentration

Source: Zhao et al. (2014)

Besides, the accumulation of Cd in *Indica* rice cultivars tends to be greater than in *Japonica* cultivars that have adjusted to the temperate environment of the region, although there is considerable variation across cultivars. Some vegetables such as carrots, leafy green vegetables, brassica plants, and solanaceous vegetables are more likely to accumulate the Cd from acidic soils, increasing the dietary intake of Cd of the local population.

According to a 2013 report by the Guangzhou Food and Drug Administration, the cadmium (Cd) levels in 44.44 per cent of sampled rice and related rice products exceeded the national quality standards, sparking widespread panic (Bi et al., 2013). Table 4.4 lists the Cd concentrations in the soil and rice samples in different regions (Lu et al., 2015). The national threshold value of food safety for Cd is 0.2 mg kg^{-1} (Zeng et al., 2015). Almost all the samples listed in Table 4.4 exceed that value. Combining the crop production data and crops' heavy metal pollution ratios of China's 32 provinces, Zhang et al. (2015) found that 13.86 per cent of the grain was affected by heavy metal pollution. This is higher than the pollution level of arable land (10.18 per cent). The reason for such high levels of heavy metal pollution in grain is likely to be that most grain is produced in southern China due to its better climate and abundant water supply to support crop growth. This is also the region where heavy metal pollution is more prevalent. Indeed, Bi et al. (2013) found that most Cd-contaminated rice comes

Table 4.4 Concentration of Cd in soil and rice in different regions (1992–2013)

Area	Cd in soil (mg kg^{-1})	Cd in rice (mg kg^{-1})
Xingtang, Hebei	4.78	0.5
Shenyang, Liaoning	4.09	0.1–0.4
Dayu, Jiangxi	1.95	0.07–1.55
Guangxi 1	16.0	0.95
Guangxi 2	10.0	0.30
Guangxi 3	3.6	0.19
Middle Hunan	8.30	1.29
Lanzhou, Gansu	9.69	0.72
Guangzhou, Guangdong	6.67	0.80
Yunnan	1.52	0.64
Zhejiang	6.69	1.17
Yanghe River, Hebei	1.56	–
Coastal area of Southern Bohai Sea	0.14	–

Source: Lu et al. (2015)

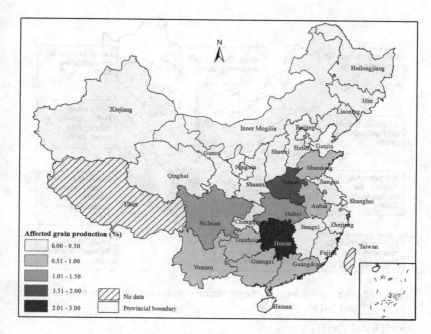

Figure 4.11 Percentages of affected grain production in each province accounting for the total grain production in China

Source: Zhang et al. (2015)

from the provinces of Hunan and Jiangxi, two of China's most important grain-producing regions. Zhang et al. (2015) found that the provinces with the highest percentage of affected grain are Hunan, Henan, Hubei and Sichuan (Figure 4.11).

China has been experiencing severe heavy metal contamination since the 1950s, and the number of reported incidents increased in the last few years, which further harmed China's public health and its economy (Lu et al., 2015). These disasters happened mostly due to insufficient safety standards in open-pit mining and smelting processes. The ten most serious contamination events of the decade from 2005 to 2015 are highlighted in Figure 4.12 (Lu et al., 2015).

Hunan Province is one of the most important regions for food production. Yet Hunan Province is particularly affected by heavy metal pollution. Nonferrous metal mining activities produce approximately 50 million tons of waste every year, which contain a large concentration of heavy metals

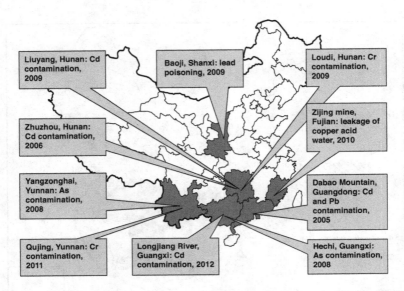

Figure 4.12 The ten most severe heavy metal contamination events between 2005 and 2015

Source: Lu et al. (2015)

(Meng, 2014). In addition, incidents regularly occur as a result of intensive mining activities, which cause the contamination of soil and water by heavy metals, leading to a dramatic drop or even the total loss of crop yields, the effects of which are felt for years (Lu et al., 2015). According to unofficial data, the concentration of heavy metals in the soil in south-central Hunan Province is more than 1,500 times the maximum safe concentration. Of the heavy metals identified in the soil, cadmium (Cd) levels were 200 times more than the levels specified in the environmental quality standards of China (Meng, 2014). For example, in 1985, the collapse of a tailing dam of a lead-zinc mine in Chenzhou (Hunan Province) led to the spread of a 15-cm thick layer of mining waste on a 400-m wide strip of farmland on both sides of the Dong River. Although immediate soil remediation was conducted in some places after the accident, Liu et al.'s 2005 study still showed unusually high levels of heavy metal contamination 20 years after the incident. As and Cd levels exceeded the thresholds set by the Chinese regulations (GB15618, 1995) by 24 and 13 times, respectively, and the contamination levels in the vegetables were 6.6 and 8.5 times the acceptable values, respectively.

Pesticide food poisoning

Pesticides harm the land by killing beneficial insect species, soil microorganisms, and worms that naturally control pest populations and keep the soil healthy. Pesticides can also damage the roots and immune systems of plants and reduce the essential nitrogen and phosphorus content of the soil (Riah et al., 2014). In addition, pesticides can leach into the broader environment through excessive application, the disposal of contaminated waste, and incineration or with water runoff after application.

In China, the use of pesticides has grown at an exponential rate over the last decades (Figure 4.13). The increased usage of pesticides has resulted in a growing amount of pesticide residue in food (Zhang et al., 2011). Most pesticides are poisons, and long-term exposure in humans can have major health effects, including damage to the liver, kidney, thyroid gland, bladder, and the central nervous system, as well as serious reproductive problems (Zhang et al., 2011). Environmental pollution, especially pollution caused by pesticide chemicals, is one of the gravest threats to China's food safety, and despite the country's improved food safety

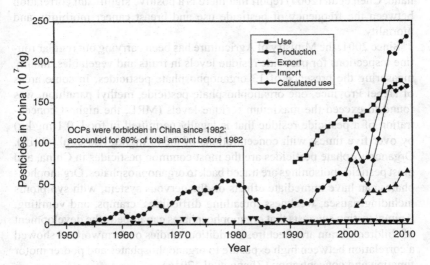

Figure 4.13 Historical production, use, export and import amounts of pesticides (1950–2011)

Note: "Use" in the figure is compiled from the China Rural Statistical Yearbook (NBSC, 2011), whereas the "calculated use" is calculated from the production, export, and import from the China Economic Yearbook (NBSC, 2012).

Source: Grung et al. (2015)

levels, contamination incidents continue to occur. Mo (2016) reports that Europe's Rapid Alert System for Food and Feed counted 3,706 Chinese food safety cases from 2002 to 2012, and that for five consecutive years China ranked first place among the 144 countries and regions monitored. A survey in 2014 showed that Chinese consumers paid close attention to food safety and that only 13 percent were satisfied with the food safety situation. Pollution caused by microorganisms was the major reason for food poisoning and related deaths, followed by pesticides and veterinary drugs (Mo, 2016).

According to a report by the World Health Organization (WHO) and United Nations Environment Programme (UNEP), there are over 26 million cases of human pesticide poisoning worldwide that are responsible for nearly 220,000 deaths every year (Zhang et al., 2011). In the United States, 67,000 cases of human pesticide poisoning are reported every year. By comparison, in China, this number reaches 500,000, with 100,000 people dying of pesticide poisoning per year. Depending on the level of exposure, less severe cases of pesticide poisoning can lead to various diseases. Cancer cases originating from pesticide poisoning are estimated to account for nearly 10 per cent of the total cancer cases (Zhang et al., 2011). On the other hand, Chen et al. (2004) report that there is a positive significant correlation between the frequency of pesticide use and breast cancer morbidity and mortality.

Since 2001, the Ministry of Agriculture has been carrying out regular routine inspections for pesticide residue levels in fruits and vegetables, mainly measuring the presence of 13 organophosphate pesticides. In some areas of Hebei Province, one organophosphate pesticide, methyl parathion, was found to exceed the maximum residue levels (MRL, the highest concentration of a pesticide residue that is legally permitted in food, 0.1 mg/kg) by over five times, with concentrations of 0.540 mg/kg (Lu et al., 2015). Organophosphate pesticides are the most common pesticides in China, and most pesticide poisonings are traced back to organophosphates. Organophosphates can have immediate effects on the nervous system, with symptoms including nausea, weakness, breathing difficulties, cramps, and vomiting. Animal testing suggests that organophosphates can impede the development of children's brain architecture. In addition, studies on farmworkers showed a correlation between high exposure to organophosphates and poorer motor function and concentration (Zhang et al., 2016).

Many pesticides are non-biodegradable, which means that a significant portion of pesticide residues remain and accumulate in the soil for years. One notorious example is DDT (dichlorodiphenyltrichloroethane), a pesticide which was used from the 1940s to the 1990s, when it was banned in most countries. DDT is just one of the many organic (carbon-based)

Table 4.5 Environmental persistency of some organochlorine pesticides

Pesticide	Required time for 5% residual (years)	Mean (years)
DDT	4~30	10
Dieldrin	5~25	8
Lindane	3~10	6.5
Chlordane	3~5	4
Telodrin	2~7	4
Heptachlor	3~5	3.5
Aldrin	1~6	3

Source: Zhang et al. (2011)

substances belonging to a group of toxic chemicals called "persistent organic pollutants", which can stay in the environment for years or decades after they were initially used. It takes on average ten years to decompose 95 per cent of DDT, with a range of four to 30 years (Table 4.5; all pesticides listed in the table are now banned in most countries). Other organochlorine pesticides are almost as persistent. Since organochlorine pesticides break down very slowly in fatty tissue, they can accumulate in the body and can be passed along the food chain. For example, studies have shown that when an animal eats a fish polluted with an organochlorine pesticide, the substance will be transferred to the animal which has consumed it (Boada et al., 2014). For this reason, organochlorine pesticides can also spread over large distances, and DDT has been found in places as distant as Antarctica.

Cancer villages

The term "cancer cluster" is defined as a "greater-than-expected number of cancer cases that occur within a group of people in a geographic area over a period of time [. . . and] is largely due to cancer-causing chemicals" (CDC, 2013). In China, digestive and respiratory cancers such as hepatic cancer, lung cancer, esophageal cancer, and stomach cancer are common illnesses among people living in these cancer villages (Lu et al., 2015). In the heavily polluted regions of China, cancer villages seem to appear in clusters. Their origins go back to the economic reforms of the 1980s, when the government encouraged the development of township and village enterprises. Some of these enterprises became a significant source of pollution, especially in the provinces of Hebei, Henan, and Shandong (Lu et al., 2015). Indeed, China's cancer villages first appeared in the 1980s

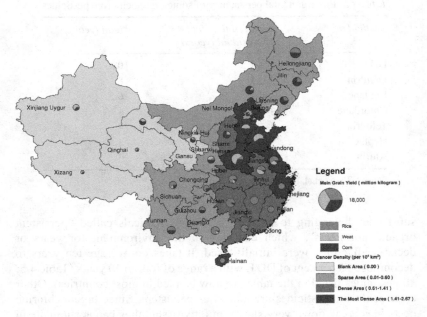

Figure 4.14 Distribution of cancer villages and grain yields in China
Source: Lu et al. (2015)

and showed a sharp increase in the 1990s, and their numbers continued to grow well into the 2000s.

When comparing the regional distribution of crop production across provinces with the geographical distribution of cancer villages, the analysis reveals that the areas with high cancer rates are also located along China's most important grain-producing regions (Figure 4.14). The major rice production areas of Jiangsu, Anhui, Jiangxi, Hunan, Hubei, and Guangdong Provinces, the wheat-production areas of Hebei, Henan, Shandong, and Jiangsu Provinces, and the maize-production areas of Hebei, Henan, and Shandong Provinces are those with the greatest concentration of cancer villages (Lu et al., 2015). According to Lu et al. (2015), 57.8 per cent of the total national grain production comes from the provinces that have the highest numbers of cancer villages, while the rice yield in these areas accounts for 64.8 per cent of the total rice yield, the wheat yield for 81 per cent of the total wheat production, and maize yield for 41.2 per cent of the total maize yield of the country (Lu et al., 2015).

Conclusion

This chapter described the direct and indirect impacts of soil degradation and pollution, which have caused significant damages to the ecosystem and people's health. Soil degradation processes consist mainly of soil acidification, soil salinification, and desertification and result in the loss of nutrients and a substantial reduction of crop yields. Soil degradation occurs mainly in the arid north and the mountainous areas in the west, where it has direct environmental (such as landslides and flooding) and economic (such as lower incomes from livestock raising) impacts. However, it also has important nationwide impacts, including dust storms, floods, and the siltation of dams. Furthermore, there is a growing risk that a reduction in grain and livestock output may raise the price of food beyond what is socially acceptable.

Soil pollution is the result of industrial activities and the excessive application of pesticides. Data on soil pollution has been so closely guarded that it has been officially categorized as a "state secret." It was only in February 2013 that the Ministry of Environmental Protection (MEP) acknowledged that "cancer villages" existed, and in 2014 it finally issued a report about the status of China's soils (He, 2014). Even though soil pollution is often invisible, it is very harmful to people's health. Through the ingestion of polluted food, it poses as serious a threat to human health as air and water pollution, which are more widely covered by the media (Delang, 2016a, 2016b). It should be noted that the impacts of soil degradation are not unknown to Chinese people, but the problem of soil pollution has been given less public attention.

The next chapter will detail the government's responses and solutions to these soil problems. These include efforts to prevent soil degradation and restore degraded soils, as well as attempts to control and eliminate the pollutants in soils.

Bibliography

Barker, A. V., & Pilbeam, D. J. (Eds.). (2015). *Handbook of Plant Nutrition*. Boca Raton (FL): CRC Press.

Bi, X., Pan, X., & Zhou, S. (2013). Soil security is alarming in China's main grain producing areas. *Environmental Science & Technology, 47*(14), 7593–7594.

Boada, L. D., Sangil, M., Álvarez-León, E. E., Hernández-Rodríguez, G., Henríquez-Hernández, L. A., Camacho, M., Zumbado, M., Serra-Majem, L., & Luzardo, O. P. (2014). Consumption of foods of animal origin as determinant of contamination by organochlorine pesticides and polychlorobiphenyls: Results from a population-based study in Spain. *Chemosphere, 114*, 121–128.

CDC. (2013). Cancer Clusters. NCEH (National Center for Environmental Health), US Centers for Disease Control and Prevention (CDC). Retrieved from www.cdc.gov/nceh/clusters/

102   *Impacts of soil degradation and pollution*

Chen, H., Zheng, C. R., Tu, C., & Zhu, Y. G. (1999). Heavy metal pollution in soils in China: Status and countermeasures. *Ambio, 28*(2), 130–134.

Chen, J. (2007). Rapid urbanization in China: A real challenge to soil protection and food security. *Catena, 69*(1), 1–15.

Chen, J. P., Lin, G., & Zhou, B. S. (2004). Correlation between pesticides exposure and morbidity and mortality of breast cancer. *Chinese Journal of Public Health-Shenyang, 20*, 289–290.

Chen, X. Y. (June, 2016). The outstanding problems of China's soils (in Chinese). China Fertilizer Network (www.fert.cn). Retrieved from www.fert.cn/news/2016/6/28/201662813395577977.shtml

Chen, Y., & Fischer, G. (1998). *A New Digital Georeferenced Database of Grassland in China.* Interim Report IR-98–062. Luxenburg (Austria): International Institute for Applied Systems Analysis. Retrieved from http://citeseerx.ist.psu.edu/viewdoc/download?doi=10.1.1.41.102&rep=rep1&type=pdf

Clever, J., & Ma, J. (2014). China's Maximum Levels for Contaminants in Foods. USDA Foreign Agricultural Services. Global Agricultural Information Network. GAIN Report Number CH14058 (Dated 12/11/2014). Retrieved from http://gain.fas.usda.gov

Delang, C. O. (2016a). *China's Air Pollution Problems.* London: Routledge.

Delang, C. O. (2016b). *China's Water Pollution Problems.* London: Routledge.

Delang, C. O., & Wang, W. (2013). Chinese forest policy reforms after 1998: The case of the Natural Forest Protection Program and Slope Land Conversion Program. *International Forestry Review, 15*(3), 290–304.

Ding, J. (2010). Chinese soil experts warn of massive threat to food security. *SciDev. Net.* Retrieved 15 December 2016 from www.scidev.net/global/earth-science/news/chinese-soil-experts-warn-of-massive-threat-to-food-security.html

Duan, X., Xie, Y., Ou, T., & Lu, H. (2011). Effects of soil erosion on long-term soil productivity in the black soil region of northeastern China. *Catena, 87*(2), 268–275.

Economy, E. C. (2011). *The River Runs Black: The Environmental Challenge to China's Future.* Ithaca, NY: Cornell University Press.

Feng, Q., Ma, H., Jiang, X. M., Wang, X., & Cao, S. X. (2015). What has caused desertification in China? *Scientific Reports, 5.* DOI: 10.1038/srep15998

Ford, P. (July, 2011). China's farmers see hope in effort to stem soil erosion caused by Three Gorges Dam. *The Christian Science Monitor.* Retrieved from www.csmonitor.com/World/Asia-Pacific/2011/0727/China-s-farmers-see-hope-in-effort-to-stem-soil-erosion-caused-by-Three-Gorges-Dam

Gao, J. H., Jia, J., Kettner, A. J., Xing, F., Wang, Y. P., Li, J., Bai, F., Zou, X., & Gao, S. (2015). Reservoir-induced changes to fluvial fluxes and their downstream impacts on sedimentary processes: The Changjiang (Yangtze) River, China. *Quaternary International,* 1–11. Retrieved from http://dx.doi.org/10.1016/j.quaint.2015.03.015

Gao, P., Wang, Z. Y., & Siegel, D. (2015). Spatial and temporal sedimentation changes in the Three Gorges Reservoir of China. *Lakes & Reservoirs: Research & Management, 20*(4), 233–242.

Gilbert, N. (February, 2010). Acid soil threatens Chinese farms. *Nature.* Retrieved 15 December 2016 from www.nature.com/news/2010/100211/full/news.2010.67.html

Greenway, H., & Munns, R. (1980). Mechanisms of salt tolerance in nonhalophytes. *Annual Review of Plant Physiology, 31*(1), 149–190.

Grung, M., Lin, Y., Zhang, H., Steen, A. O., Huang, J., Zhang, G., & Larssen, T. (2015). Pesticide levels and environmental risk in aquatic environments in China: A review. *Environment International, 81*, 87–97.

Guo, J. H., Liu, X. J., Zhang, Y., Shen, J. L., Han, W. X., Zhang, W. F., Christie, P., Goulding, K. W., Vitousek, P. M., & Zhang, F. S. (2010). Significant acidification in major Chinese croplands. *Science, 327*(5968), 1008–1010.

GYGA. (2016). Global Yield Gap Atlas: China. Retrieved from www.yieldgap.org/china

Hao, N. (June, 2016). *Country Makes Gains in Fight against Desertification*. Beijing: The State Council of the People's Republic of China. Retrieved 15 December 2016 from http://english.gov.cn/news/top_news/2016/06/17/content_281475373692880.htm

He, G. (June, 2014). China's dirty pollution secret: The boom poisoned its soil and crops. *Yale Environment 360*. Retrieved 15 December 2016 from http://e360.yale.edu/feature/chinas_dirty_pollution_secret_the_boom_poisoned_its_soil_and_crops/2782/

Ho, M.-W. (2010). China's Soils Ruined by Overuse of Chemical Fertilizers. Institute of Science and Society, Report 30/03/10. Retrieved from www.i-sis.org.uk/chinasSoilRuined.php

Hornby, L. (September, 2015). Chinese environment: Ground operation. *Financial Times*. Retrieved from www.ft.com/content/d096f594-4be0-11e5-b558-8a9722977189

Hou, E. Q., Wen, D. Z., Li, J. L., Zuo, W. D., Zhang, L. L., Kuang, Y. W., & Li, J. (2012). Soil acidity and exchangeable cations in remnant natural and plantation forests in the urbanized Pearl River Delta, China. *Soil Research, 50*(3), 207–215. Retrieved from http://dx.doi.org/10.1071/SR11344

Huang, R. Q., & Li, W. L. (2011). Formation, distribution and risk control of landslides in China. *Journal of Rock Mechanics and Geotechnical Engineering, 3*(2), 97–116.

Hvistendahl, M. (February, 2010). Fertilizer is acidifying Chinese land. *Science Mag*. Retrieved from www.sciencemag.org/news/2010/02/fertilizer-acidifying-chinese-land

Jie, D. (August, 2010). Chinese soil experts warn of massive threat to food security. *SciDev.Net*. Retrieved 15 December 2016 from www.scidev.net/global/earth-science/news/chinese-soil-experts-warn-of-massive-threat-to-food-security.html

LADA. (October, 2010). *China National Level Report of Land Degradation Assessment in Drylands*. Prepared by: LADA Project Team, P. R. China. Rome: FAO.

Lars, J. (2003). Hazards of heavy metal contamination. *British Medical Bulletin, 68*(1), 167–182.

Li, Y. X., Yu, Y., Yang, Z. F., Shen, Z. Y., Wang, X., & Cai, Y. P. (2016). A comparison of metal distribution in surface dust and soil among super city, town, and rural area. *Environmental Science and Pollution Research, 23*(8), 7849–7860. DOI: 10.1007/s11356-015-5911-7

Li, Y. X., Zhang, W. F., Ma, L., Wu, L., Shen, J. B., Davies, W. J., Oenema, O. Zhang, F., & Dou, Z. (2013). An analysis of China's grain production: Looking back and looking forward. *Food and Energy Security, 3*(1), 19–32. DOI: 10.1002/fes3.41

Li, Y. Y., Wang, H. B., Wang, H. J., Yin, F., Yang, X. Y., & Hu, Y. J. (2014). Heavy metal pollution in vegetables grown in the vicinity of amulti-metal mining area in Gejiu, China: Total concentrations, speciation analysis, and health risk. *Environmental Science and Pollution Research, 21*(21), 12569–12582. DOI: 10.1007/s11356–014–3188-x

Liu, C., Wang, X., Yin, M., Hou, H., & Dong, H. (2014). Risk analysis and stability assessment on the suspended river of the lower reaches of the Yellow River. *Journal of Clean Energy Technologies, 2*(2), 187–190.

Liu, H., Probst, A., & Liao, B. (2005). Metal contamination of soils and crops affected by the Chenzhou lead/zinc mine spill (Hunan, China). *Science of the Total Environment, 339*(1), 153–166.

Liu, J., & Diamond, J. (2005). China's environment in a globalizing world. *Nature, 435*(7046), 1179–1186.

Lorenz, R. D., Balme, M. R., Gu, Z. L., Henrik, K., Klose, M., Kurgansky, M. V., Patel, M. R., Reiss, D., Rossi, A. P., Spiga, A., Takemi, T., & Wei, W. (2016). History and applications of dust devil studies. *Space Science Reviews*, 1–33. DOI: 10.1007/ s11214-016-0239-2

Lu, J. Y., & Chen, G. (2013). Impact of soil erosion on rural poverty. *Asia Agricultural Research, 5*(2), 21–25.

Lu, Y. L., Song, S., Wang, R. S., Liu, Z. Y., Meng, J., Sweetman, A. J., Jenkins, A., Ferrier, R. C., Li, H., Luo, W., & Wang, T. (2015). Impacts of soil and water pollution on food safety and health risks in China. *Environment International, 77*, 5–15.

Luo, G., Chu, T., Yan, C., Liu, H., Wen, Y., & Zhang, L. (1997). The stability of the suspended river on the lower reaches of the Yellow River and its geo-environmental study. *Geological Review, 4*, 441–448.

Lyn, T. E. (February, 2010). Nitrogen-laden fertilizer said to ruin some China croplands. *Shanghai Daily*. Retrieved from www.shanghaidaily.com/nation/Nitrogenladen-fertilizer-said-to-ruin-some-China-croplands/shdaily.shtml

McKersie, B. D., & Lesheim, Y. (2013). *Stress and Stress Coping in Cultivated Plants*. Heidelberg: Springer Science & Business Media.

Mao, R. Z., Fitzpatrick, R. W., Liu, X. J., & Davies, P. J. (2002). Chemical Properties of Selected Soils from the North China Plain. Regional Water and Soil Assessment for Managing Sustainable Agriculture in China and Australia, ACIAR Monograph No. 84, 173–186. Retrieved 15 December 2016 from www.eoc.csiro. au/aciar/book/PDF/Monograph_84_Chapter_13.pdf

Meng, A. (December, 2014). Heavy metal pollution in Hunan soil exceeds China's limits by 1,500 times. *South China Morning Post*. Retrieved 15 December 2016 from www.scmp.com/news/china/article/1653877/heavy-metal-pollution-hunan-soil-exceeds-chinas-limits-1500-times

MEP. (2003). *The Temporary Regulation of Ecological Function Zoning*. Beijing: Ministry of Environmental Protection. Retrieved 15 December 2016 from http:// sts.mep.gov.cn/stbh/stglq/200308/t20030815_90755.shtml

Mo, H. (2016). Pesticides pose major threat to China's food safety: Report. *ECNS Wire*. Retrieved 15 December 2016 from www.ecns.cn/cns-wire/2016/01-28/197427.shtml

Mofcom. (March, 2009). *Geographical Features of the People's Republic of China*. Beijing: Ministry of Commerce. Retrieved 15 December 2016 from http://no2. mofcom.gov.cn/article/aboutchina/geography/200903/20090306117654.shtml

NBSC. (2011). *China Rural Statistical Yearbooks, 1991–2010*. Beijing: National Bureau of Statistics of China.

NBSC. (2012). *China Economic Yearbooks, 1950–2011*. Beijing: National Bureau of Statistics of China.

Pan, X. C., & Liu, J. (2011). Study on health effects of dust storms (Asian dusts) in China. *Epidemiology, 22*(1), S26–S27.

Pimentel, D., & Burgess, M. (2013). Soil erosion threatens food production. *Agriculture, 3*(3), 443–463.

Ran, L., Lu, X. X., Xin, Z., & Yang, X. (2013). Cumulative sediment trapping by reservoirs in large river basins: A case study of the Yellow River basin. *Global and Planetary Change, 100*, 308–319.

Riah, W., Laval, K., Laroche-Ajzenberg, E., Mougin, C., Latour, X., & Trinsoutrot-Gattin, I. (2014). Effects of pesticides on soil enzymes: A review. *Environmental Chemistry Letters, 12*(2), 257–273.

Salama, R. B., Otto, C. J., & Fitzpatrick, R. W. (1999). Contributions of ground-water conditions to soil and water salinization. *Hydrogeology Journal, 7*(1), 46–64.

SFA. (2011). *A Bulletin of Status Quo of Desertification and Sandification in China*. Beijing: State Forestry Administration. Retrieved from www.documentcloud.org/documents/1237947-state-forestry-administration-desertification.html

Shangguan, W., Dai, Y., Liu, B., Zhu, A., Duan, Q., Wu, L., Ji, D., Ye, A., Yuan, H., & Zhang, Q. (2013). A China data set of soil properties for land surface modeling. *Journal of Advances in Modeling Earth Systems, 5*(2), 212–224.

Su, C., Jiang, L. Q., & Zhang, W. J. (2014). A review on heavy metal contamination in the soil worldwide: Situation, impact and remediation techniques. *Environmental Skeptics and Critics, 3*(2), 24–38.

UBC International Reporting Program. (2016). China's Generation Green. Retrieved from http://projects.thestar.com/chinas-generation-green/

UN. (2016a). *On Day to Combat Desertification, UN Calls for Action to Restore Land Resources*. New York: United Nations. Retrieved from www.un.org/apps/news/story.asp?NewsID=54255#.V-3QXckUj3Y

UNESCO. (2003). Environmental consequences of desertification. In: *Learning to Combat Desertification*. New York: Unesco, Ch. 11. Retrieved 15 December 2016 from http://unesdoc.unesco.org/images/0012/001258/125816e.pdf

Vidal, J. (September, 2009). Dust storms spread deadly diseases worldwide. *The Guardian*. Retrieved 15 December 2016 from www.theguardian.com/world/2009/sep/27/dust-storms-diseases-sydney

Wang, G., Wu, B., & Wang, Z. Y. (2005). Sedimentation problems and manage-ment strategies of Sanmenxia Reservoir, Yellow River, China. *Water Resources Research, 41*(9), W09417, 1–17.

Wang, P., Dong, S., & Lassoie, J. P. (2013). *The Large Dam Dilemma: An Explora-tion of the Impacts of Hydro Projects on People and the Environment in China*. Heidelberg: Springer Science & Business Media.

Wang, Y. (2014). Polluted farmland leads to Chinese food security fears. *China Dia-logue*. Retrieved 15 December 2016 from www.chinadialogue.net/article/show/single/en/6636-Polluted-farmland-leads-to-Chinese-food-security-fears

Wang, Z. Y., Lee, J. H., & Melching, C. S. (2015). *River Dynamics and Integrated River Management*. Heidelberg: Springer, Ch. 6, pp. 337–395.

Warrence, N. J., Pearson, K. E., & Bauder, J. W. (2003). *Basics of Salinity and Sodicity Effects on Soil Physical Properties*. Bozeman (MT): Department of Land Resources and Environmental Sciences, Montana State University-. Retrieved 15 December 2016 from http://waterquality.montana.edu/energy/cbm/background/soil-prop.html

Watts, J. (June, 2012). The clean-up begins on China's dirty secret: Soil pollution. *The Guardian*. Retrieved 15 December 2016 from www.theguardian.com/environment/2012/jun/12/china-soil-pollution-bonn-challenge

Wei, X., Zhang, Z., Shi, P. J., Wang, P., Chen, Y., Song, X., & Tao, F. (2015). Is yield increase sufficient to achieve food security in China? *PLoS One, 10*(2), e0116430. DOI: 10.1371/journal.pone.0116430

Wu, R. G., Tiessen, H., & Chen, Z. (2008). The impacts of pasture degradation on soil nutrients and plant compositions in Alpine Grassland, China. *Agricultural, Food, and Environmental Sciences, 2*(2), 1–14.

Xia, X., Dong, J., Wang, M., Xie, H., Xia, N., Li, H., Zhang, X., Mou, X., Wen, J., & Bao, Y. (2016). Effect of water-sediment regulation of the Xiaolangdi reservoir on the concentrations, characteristics, and fluxes of suspended sediment and organic carbon in the Yellow River. *Science of the Total Environment, 571*, 487–497.

Xu, W. (April, 2016). Report forecasts first drop in wheat production for 12 years. *China Daily*. Retrieved 15 December 2016 from www.chinadaily.com.cn/china/2016-04/22/content_24755828.htm

Yang, J. (July, 2006). Recent Evolution of Soil Salinization in China and Its Driving Processes. Presentation at the 18th Word Congress of Soil Science, Philadelphia, Pennsylvania, 9–15 July 2016. Retrieved 15 December 2016 from www.ldd.go.th/18wcss/techprogram/P13368.HTM

Yang, X., Zhang, K., Jia, B., & Ci, L. (2005). Desertification assessment in China: An overview. *Journal of Arid Environments, 63*(2), 517–531.

Yardley, J. (November, 2007). Chinese dam projects criticized for their human costs. *New York Times*. Retrieved 15 December 2016 from www.nytimes.com/2007/11/19/world/asia/19dam.html?_r=0

Zeng, F., Wei, W., Li, M., Huang, R., Yang, F., & Duan, Y. (2015). Heavy metal contamination in rice-producing soils of Hunan Province, China and potential health risks. *International Journal of Environmental Research and Public Health, 12*(12), 15584–15593.

Zhang, G. (2016). Characteristics of Runoff Nutrient Loss and Particle Size Distribution of Eroded Sediment under Varied Rainfall Intensities. 4th International Conference on Machinery, Materials and Computing Technology (ICMMCT 2016). Retrieved 15 December 2016 from www.atlantis-press.com/php/download_paper.php?id=25850018

Zhang, W. J., Jiang, F. B., & Ou, J. F. (2011). Global pesticide consumption and pollution: With China as a focus. *Proceedings of the International Academy of Ecology and Environmental Sciences, 1*(2), 125–144.

Zhang, X., Wu, M., Yao, H., Yang, Y., Cui, M., Tu, Z., Stallones L., & Xiang, H. (2016). Pesticide poisoning and neurobehavioral function among farm workers in Jiangsu, People's Republic of China. *Cortex, 74*, 396–404.

Zhang, X. Y., Zhong, T. Y., Liu, L., & Ouyang, X. Y. (2015). Impact of soil heavy metal pollution on food safety in China. *PLoS One, 10*(8), e0135182. DOI: 10.1371/journal.pone.0135182

Zhang, Z. Y., Abuduwaili, J. L. L., & Yimit, H. (2014). The occurrence, sources and spatial characteristics of soil salt and assessment of soil salinization risk in Yanqi Basin, Northwest China. *PLoS One, 9*(9), e106079. DOI: 10.1371/journal.pone.0106079

Zhao, F. J., Ma, Y. B., Zhu, Y. G., Tang, Z., & McGrath, S. P. (2014). Soil contamination in China: Current status and mitigation strategies. American Chemical Society. *Environmental Science & Technology, 49*(2), 750–759. DOI: 10.1021/es5047099

Zhou, Q. X., Teng, Y., & Liu, Y. (2016). A study on soil-environmental quality criteria and standards of arsenic. *Applied Geochemistry* (Available online 10 May 2016). Retrieved from http://dx.doi.org/10.1016/j.apgeochem.2016.05.001

Zhuang, P., Zou, H. L., & Shu, W. S. (2009). Biotransfer of heavy metals along a soil-plant-insect-chicken food chain: Field study. *Journal of Environmental Sciences, 21*(6), 849–853.

5 The solutions to soil degradation and soil pollution

Introduction

Eliminating soil degradation and soil pollution require markedly different solutions. Soil degradation necessitates efforts to stop the degradation, followed by the restoration of the topsoil. In most cases, the degradation is caused by excessive use of the land, so the restoration process involves withdrawing it from farming or herding activities and planting vegetation on the soil. One of the difficulties lies in determining what vegetation needs to be planted. China being a very large country, soil restoration policies should be focused on the particular climate, precipitation, and soil conditions of the different areas. However, China also being centrally planned, the policies are not always properly focused to the conditions and requirements of the individual areas.

Removing the pollutants from the soil, on the other hand, requires more concerted efforts. These efforts will inevitably be more expensive. As mentioned in Chapter 2, soil pollution is more difficult to identify because it is not visible to the naked eye. The rehabilitation of polluted soil is a major challenge, especially if the pollutants are heavy metals. Polluted air is blown away and polluted water flows down rivers, so if the emissions stop, the pollutants in the air and water will dilute. On the other hand, pollutants in the soil will remain there for decades, if not treated. This means that efforts and expenses to alleviate the soil pollution problems may eventually far exceed those made to address air and water pollution (Delang, 2016a, 2016b). As Zhuang Guotai, the head of the Ministry of Environmental Protection's Department of Nature and Ecology Conservation, said, "In comparison with efforts to clean up air and water pollution, we've hardly got started with soil. But once the market is opened up, soil remediation will be on a far bigger scale than either air or water cleanup" (He, 2014a).

In this chapter, I describe the solutions to soil degradation and soil pollution. Efforts to alleviate soil degradation, as hinted at earlier, focus mainly on reverting the degraded land to non-extractive uses, usually the original vegetation (forest or grassland) or more sustainable forms of agriculture.

Efforts to control soil pollution are more complicated. The first step toward addressing soil pollution is to identify the polluted soil and the enterprises that are responsible for the pollution. The second step is to develop and enforce laws to pressure the polluting enterprises to stop their discharge activities. The third step is to apply technologies to reduce the pollution. Existing technologies are expensive, so China is also making an effort to develop cheaper technologies, given the extent of the problem (20 million ha of arable land is contaminated) and the likely costs involved (up to CNY 11 trillion).

Land degradation prevention and control measures

The tasks ahead, in terms of the rehabilitation of China's degraded land, are quite enormous. Since the 1990s, each year, over 1.5 million ha of previously unaffected land has succumbed to wind and water erosion. The amount of soil loss has exceeded 300 million metric tons, and China now has to rehabilitate 295 million ha of land that are affected by erosion, including 24 million ha of slope farmland and 960,000 erosion gullies. It also has to protect the black soil in northeast China and stop desertification in the north. While rehabilitating eroded soil is already a colossal task, the trend toward increasing erosion attributable to human activities has yet to be effectively addressed (MWR, 2016). The accomplishments so far, even though there have been valuable attempts at stopping degradation and restoring land, fall far short of the country's overall objectives for ecological restoration and evolving toward a sustainable economy.

Legal and policy system

The development and implementation of environmental laws in China date back to 1979, when the first law related to environmental protection was passed (Table 5.1). The first law dealing with soil protection was adopted in

Table 5.1 List of main soil-related laws

Note	Name	Adopted	Went into effect
1	Environmental Protection Law	1979–09–13	1979–09–13
2	Forestry Law	1984–09–20	1985–01–01
3	Grassland Law	1985–06–18	1985–10–01
4	Law on Water and Soil Conservation	1991–06–29	1991–06–29
5	Law on Prevention and Control of Desertification	2001–08–31	2002–01–01

Source: Mu et al. (2014)

1984, but its focus was mainly on forestry. The first law specifically targeting soil protection and intending to bring soil degradation under control, the Law of Water and Soil Conservation, was only enacted in 1991 (Mu et al., 2014). Thanks to that law, according to MWR (2016), soil and water conservation projects were initiated that helped to prevent and control over 10 million ha of land vulnerable to soil and water erosion and helped avoid the erosion of 2.24 billion metric tons of soil (MWR, 2016). Although the formulation and implementation of these laws have played an important role in China's soil protection work, there are still many deficiencies in the country's environmental legislation (Mu et al., 2014). In particular, there are problems of repetition and non-coordination among the various environmental laws and regulations. For example, prior to the revision of the "Environmental Protection Law" in 2014, 31 of its 47 articles were repeated in other environmental pollution control laws. At the same time, rules were also inconsistent in their fundamental principles and basic procedures (Mu et al., 2014), and there are still no specific laws regarding the management of toxic chemical, nature conservation, and compensation for environmental damage. Technical environmental specifications and standards are also lacking. All these deficiencies result in gaps in the implementation of the laws and different levels of enforcement across regions (Mu et al., 2014).

China has also received a lot of criticism for the lack of transparency surrounding its legal system, as well as its poorly educated jurists, vaguely written laws, and ineffective enforcement (Economy, 2003). Professor Wang Jin has pinpointed that there are "no big mistakes, but also no obvious effects" in China's environmental laws and that "everything looks perfect and extensive, but it's difficult to find a specific solution to the problem in the law provisions when facing real problems" (Mu et al., 2014). According to Mu et al. (2014), the problems are rooted in the poor design of the legal code, the ambiguous roles of different authorities, the imbalance of rights and duties, and the lack of executability of the laws in the context of the legal system. Many environment-related laws suggest that it is the local governments' responsibility to protect their immediate environment, but unfortunately local governments rarely enforce the rules and regulations because of financial constraints. This resulted in a geographically heterogeneous enforcement of environmental laws.

Démurger et al. (2005)'s research investigated how the national forest protection program is enforced at the local level in three townships in northern Sichuan Province and found striking differences among the observed townships, not only in their designated firewood collection areas but also in their attitude toward the national rules and regulations. Table 5.2 shows that the understanding of the informal agreement on fuelwood collection, the infringement of forest resource use regulations, and the imposition of penalties varied

Table 5.2 Enforcement of the national forest protection program in three townships in Sichuan Province

Townships	Muzuo	Baima	Wujiao
Number of offenses reported in 2003	A few	20–30	2
Type of offense	Cutting for firewood	Logging, transport and sale of timber	Cutting for firewood
Number of forest wardens	30	4–8	80
Number of penalties imposed	1	20	2
Type of penalty	Fine (CNY 1,000)	Fine (CNY 1,000 to 2,000) + confiscation of tools	Fine (CNY 200)
Overt tolerance of offenses	–	yes	yes

Source: Démurger et al. (2005)

from one township to another. Wujiao had the largest number of forest wardens but few fines, with only two penalties imposed in 2003. Baima had less than 10 percent of the wardens that Wujiao had but imposed 10 times more fines than Wujiao during the same year (Démurger et al., 2005).

Reforestation of dryland areas

China's government first acknowledged the environmental problems of the country's dryland areas during the 1970s. In 1978, it embarked on one of the world's most ambitious environmental conservation programs with the Three-North Shelter Forest Program (also called Three-Norths Shelterbelt Program and commonly referred to as the "Great Green Wall"), scheduled to last until 2050. The program set out to plant trees on about 36.5 million ha on a 2,800-mile strip of land across northern China. The purpose of the program is to reverse the long-term consequences of desertification by planting fast-growing trees, such as aspen, which can quickly develop soil-stabilizing root systems and provide a protective canopy cover. The planting of new forests may also offer potential benefits to local economies by supplying timber or raw material for papermaking (Luoma, 2012). In addition, in 1994, the government launched a second large program in the Loess Plateau: the Loess Plateau Watershed Rehabilitation Project. Both projects had the goal of returning China's heavily degraded Loess Plateau to an area of sustainable agricultural production by boosting agricultural productivity and incomes, while also mitigating desertification.

Since the late 1980s, several other forest protection programs have been set up to preserve and promote the benefits of forest ecosystems by way of

Table 5.3 Overview of China's afforestation programs since the 1970s

Name of program	Duration	Coverage	Stated target	Achievements as of 1999
National Greening Campaign (1)	1987–present	Has varied over time	Has varied over time	27.9 billion trees planted
"Three-Norths" Shelterbelt Program	1978–2050	551 counties in 13 provinces	Afforestation of 35.08 million ha by 2050	25.67 million ha planted
Protective Afforestation Along the Upper and Middle Reaches of the Yangtze River	1989–2000	271 counties in 12 provinces	Planting and restoration of 6.75 million ha	4.8 million ha planted
Coastal Shelterbelt Development	1991–2000	195 counties in 11 provinces	Planting of 3.56 million ha	1.08 million ha planted
Cropland Protection and Agro-Forestry in the Plains	1988–2000	918 counties in 26 provinces	Set standard	850 counties reached standard
Taihang Mountain Afforestation	1990–2010	110 counties in 4 provinces	Planting of 4 million ha	3.28 million ha planted
Combating Desertification Campaign	1991–2000	598 counties in 17 provinces	Control desertification in over 7.18 million ha	Desertification controlled in 8 million ha

Notes: (1) This campaign is also called the "National Compulsory Tree-Planting Campaign".
Source: Yin et al. (2005), Table adapted from Lu et al. (2002)

watershed protection, the regulation of forest streams, erosion management, and maintenance of the biodiversity of forest ecosystems. Table 5.3 lists the forestry protection programs and their effects until 1999. Starting from the 21st century, other programs, including the "Conversion of cropland into revegetation project", the "Sand source treatment project" of Beijing and Tianjin, the "Grassland into grassland conversion project", and the "Integrated sub-watershed management project" were initiated as a series of ecological prevention and control schemes (LADA, 2010).

These projects focused on structural and ecological conservation. Structural conservation includes the construction of sediment retention dams and terrace cultivation. Ecological conservation includes the protection of mature plantations and natural forests (Figure 5.1). The programs have had

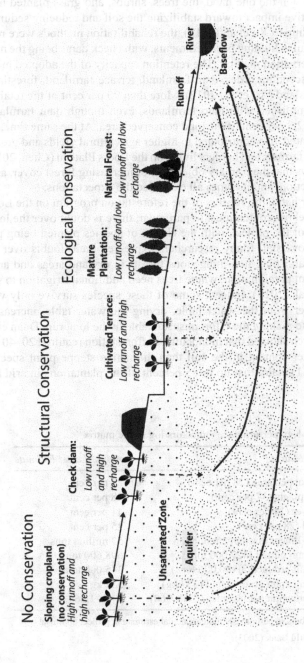

Figure 5.1 Theoretical overview of different soil conservation methods

Source: Gates et al. (2016)

mixed success. On the one hand, the trees, shrubs, and grass planted have had some positive impact toward stabilizing the soil and reducing sediment runoff. According to Xu et al. (2012), the rehabilitation methods were relatively successful in holding back sediments, with check dams being the most effective conservation method. The retention capacity of the adopted methods are, in descending order: dam farmland, terrace farmland, forestland, and lastly grassland (Xu et al., 2012). More than 90 per cent of the retained soil was accomplished with dam farmlands, even though dam farmlands occupied only 2.3 per cent of the total conserved area. At the same time, the vegetation planted also contributed to higher agricultural yields and greater incomes to the farmers and herders living on the Loess Plateau (Chen, 2013). Table 5.4 shows that the primary objectives of increasing forest cover, agricultural production, and incomes all exceeded the expectations.

On the other hand, the success of the reforestation program on the Loess Plateau is somehow contentious. In particular, there is doubt over the long-term viability of the project, with the choice of species planted being particularly controversial. Many researchers expressed their doubts over the efficacy of establishing non-indigenous forests in dryland areas and areas with insufficient precipitation, where trees need additional irrigation to survive (Feng et al., 2015). Indeed, some of these species survive only with additional water from the water table, drying the water table, increasing salinization, and making the effort unsustainable in the long run. Duan et al. (2004)'s research showed that monoculture afforestation required 20–40 per cent more water content in the soil than the native steppe plant species. Cao et al. (2011) claim that up to 85 percent of the plantations in arid and

Table 5.4 Key performance indicators/log frame matrix

Indicator/Matrix	Actual/Latest Estimate
Annual cropped area (28 per cent)	21 per cent
Perennial plants (37 per cent)	48 per cent
Forest cover (14 per cent)	41 per cent
Wasteland (28 per cent)	15 per cent
Annual sediment discharge reduction	57 million tons
Annual grain output (427,000 tons)	698,600 tons
Annual fruit production (80,000 tons)	345,000 tons
Annual per capita grain output (357 kg)	532 kg
Annual per capita net incomes (CNY 360)	CNY 1,263

Note: Numbers in parenthesis indicate actual estimate at project appraisal

Source: World Bank (2003)

semi-arid regions don't survive over the long haul. Similarly, Li (1997) argued that the survival rate of trees was only about 25 per cent on the Loess Plateau. In addition, Xu et al. (2004) found that the quality of the trees that survived was rather poor.

Another problem brought by afforestation is the damage to biodiversity. According to Cao et al. (2010), in order to satisfy the great demands of the Chinese wood industry, over 80 per cent of the country's afforestation was based on establishing monoculture plantations of fast-growing tree species that have low water-use efficiency. The biodiversity of plant species of afforested areas dropped by on average 52 per cent in northern China. Another cause for concern is the cultivation pattern of monoculture tree plantations over vast areas of land, with little biodiversity (Luoma, 2012).

In conclusion, although the country's afforestation efforts helped convert 29.1 per cent of its land area (2.2 billion ha) into forest by 2005 (Figure 5.2), the processes of land degradation and desertification also continued to escalate, indicating that these expensive reforestation strategies have produced mixed results. The deserted areas in the country have been expanding at

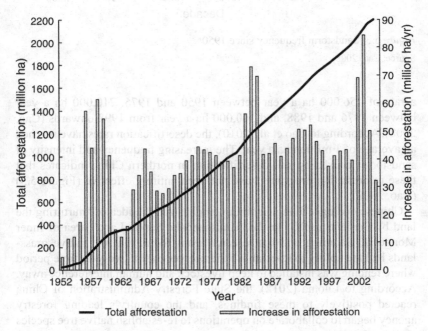

Figure 5.2 Afforestation in China (1952–2005)

Source: Cao (2008)

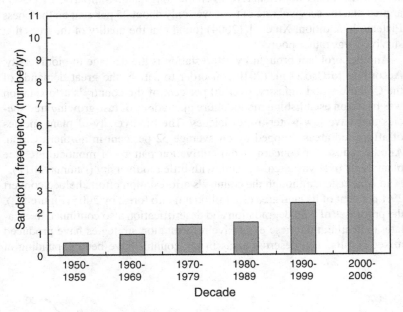

Figure 5.3 Sandstorm frequency since 1950
Source: Cao (2008)

a rate of 156,000 ha a year between 1950 and 1975, 210,000 ha a year between 1976 and 1988, and 360,000 ha a year from 1998 onwards (Cao, 2008). According to Cao et al. (2010), the desertification rates have reached an average of 1 million ha a year. The increasing frequency and intensity of sandstorms caused by soil desertification in northern China indicates that these reforestation programs have not been entirely effective (Figure 5.3) (Cao, 2008).

Chinese ecologist Jiang Gaoming emphasized the idea of "nurturing the land by the land itself". In the "Hunshandake Sandy Land" area of Inner Mongolia, Gaoming and his research team found that the native grass-lands had the ability to re-establish themselves over a two-year time period where fencing was installed to keep livestock and human interference away. According to Luoma (2012), the State Forestry Administration of China reacted positively to these findings, and the country's leading forestry agency began to collaborate on operations to re-establish native tree species (Luoma, 2012).

Natural Forest Protection Program (NFPP)

In 1998, following a series of natural disasters that had struck the country in 1997 and 1998, the State Forestry Administration (SFA) put forward the Natural Forest Protection Program (NFPP), a comprehensive scheme for preserving the natural woodlands and creating new forests (Yin et al., 2005). Specific objectives of the NFPP were to:

(1) reduce the levels of timber harvesting in natural forests from 32 million m³ to 12 million m³ between 1997 and 2003;
(2) preserve approximately 90 million ha of natural forests;
(3) replant an additional 30.97 million ha through various techniques (e.g. hand-planting seedlings, aerial seeding, and mountain closures) by 2010 (Yin et al., 2005).

The NFPP covers 17 provinces and about 68.2 million ha of forestland (Figure 5.4), including 56.4 million ha of natural forest, about 53 percent of the

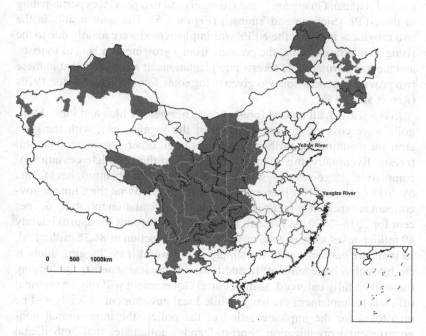

Figure 5.4 Areas in which the Natural Forest Protection Program was implemented
Source: Delang and Wang (2013)

total natural forest area. It was initially set for ten years (2000–2010), but
it was expanded for another ten years in 2010 and is now expected to last
until 2020. Since its beginning, 11 more counties have been included in the
NFPP project (Sun et al., 2016).

Ren et al. (2015) argued that China had achieved its NFPP goal. In 2000,
176.5 million ha, roughly equal to 18.7 per cent of China's mainland, was
covered with forests (12.3 per cent, with canopy cover $\geq$ 70 per cent) or
woodlands (6.4 per cent, with canopy cover < 70 per cent and tree, plus
shrub cover $\geq$ 40 per cent). Ren et al. (2015) found that since the NFPP was
introduced in 1998, the rate of forest loss across the country has declined by
1.05 per cent annually. Comparing the forest loss rates of provinces enrolled
in the NFPP with provinces where the NFPP was not implemented, they
found that the rate of loss in non-NFPP provinces was higher than that in
most NFPP provinces: by 2010, NFPP provinces had seen an annual loss
rate of forest of 0.62 per cent, compared to 2.07 per cent in non-NFPP provinces. The five provinces worst affected by deforestation were in south and
southwest China, including three provinces where NFPP was not implemented (Hunan, Guangdong, and Guangxi) and two provinces participating
in the NFPP (Sichuan and Yunnan) (Figure 5.5). The poor results in the
two provinces in which the NFPP was implemented were mainly due to the
rising standards of living, the pressure from a growing numbers of tourists,
and the transformation of forests into plantations. It also seems that in these
two provinces permission was given to log some forests planted in the 1970s
(Ren et al., 2015).

In April 2015, all natural forests across northeast China and Inner Mongolia were covered in the extension of the logging ban, with the government planning for further expansions to all other state-owned natural
forests. Eventually, this is expected to lead to the complete cessation of
commercial, large-scale logging in all the natural forests throughout China
by 2017 (Zhao, 2015). Iversen (2016) also reported that the Chinese government is expected to reduce logging quotas in plantation forests by 6.3 per
cent for 2016–2020. At present, natural forests account for approximately
49 million m^3 of China's total annual timber production of 84.38 million m^3,
so there are concerns as to the supply of softwood if the logging quota is
cut by such a large amount. In addition, it is unclear whether the logging
ban will be fully enforced, as the Central Government will rely on regional
officials to implement the bans. While local government officials will be
monitored for the implementation of the policy, the international non-
governmental organization "Forest Trends" anticipates that both illegal
and legal logging, such as forest thinning, will continue in natural forests
(Iversen, 2016).

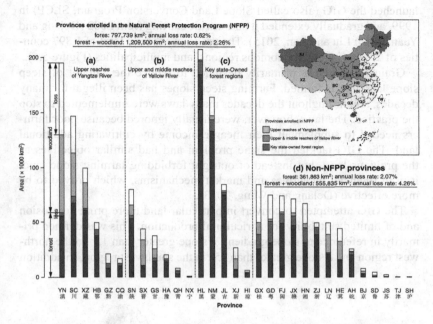

Figure 5.5 Forest (canopy cover ≥ 70 per cent) and woodland (canopy cover < 70 per cent and tree plus shrub cover ≥ 40 per cent) cover in 2000 and loss of this cover in 2000–2010 by province and by NFPP status: (a) upper reaches of the Yangtze River (26.09 million ha, loss of 0.71 per cent), (b) the upper and middle reaches of the Yellow River (10.68 million ha, loss of 0.71 per cent), (c) key state-owned forest regions (43 million ha, loss of 0.55 per cent), and (d) non-NFPP provinces (36.19 million ha, loss of 2.07 per cent). Inset shows NFPP-enrolled provinces

Note: AH, Anhui; BJ, Beijing; CQ, Chongqing; FJ, Fujian; GD, Guangdong; GS, Gansu; GX, Guangxi; GZ, Guizhou; HA, Henan; HB, Hubei; HE, Hebei; HI, Hainan; HL, Heilongjiang; HN, Hunan; JL, Jilin; JS, Jiangsu; JX, Jiangxi; LN, Liaoning; NM, Inner Mongolia; NX, Ningxia; QH, Qinghai; SC, Sichuan; SD, Shandong; SH, Shanghai; SN, Shaanxi; SX, Shanxi; TJ, Tianjin; XJ, Xinjiang; XZ, Tibet; YN, Yunnan; ZJ, Zhejiang.

Source: Ren et al. (2015)

Grain for Green (GfG)

With the introduction of the NFPP, the Chinese authorities took steps to bring the levels of timber harvesting under control and protect natural forests. However, these forest reforms did not solve the underlying issues of overgrazing and farming on slopes, which are the major contributors to soil erosion and desertification in western China. To address this problem, China launched the GfG (also called Slope Land Conversion Program, SLCP) in 1999, and gradually extended it nationwide starting from 2002 (Delang and Yuan, 2015; Liu and Lan, 2015). The program covers a total of 1,897 counties of 25 provinces, autonomous regions, and municipalities (Figure 5.6).

Grain for Green is primarily designed to reduce the amount of steep slope land that is farmed. Farming steep slopes has been illegal for many decades, and throughout the decades many laws were implemented to stop the practice. The laws, however, were usually ignored because poor farmers needed to supplement their meagre income by cultivating additional land. The GfG tackled the same problem and had similar objectives as the previous laws, but instead of outright forbidding farming slope land, it used financial incentives and market mechanisms, which proved to be more effective (Delang and Wang, 2013).

The GfG attempted to convert in particular land more prone to erosion and of limited suitability for agricultural production. This was defined primarily in reference to slope gradient: a slope greater than 15° in the northwest region and a slope greater than 25° in the southwest region. In addition

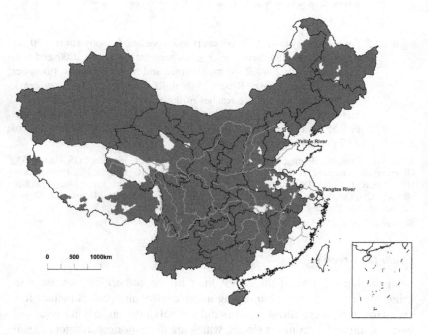

Figure 5.6 Areas of implementation of the GfG

Source: Delang and Wang (2013)

to slope land, the GfG targeted three other types of land (Hori and Kojima, 2008):

(1) Farmland, where desertification or alkalinity are severe.
(2) Farmland located in an ecologically important area, where the capacity to farm productively is low and unstable.
(3) Devastated land where soil erosion is severe.

The policy was based on the principle of raising wood on land suitable for wood, grass on land suitable for grass, and farm agricultural products on land suitable for agriculture. In other words, the land to be converted was to be covered with the original vegetation. If the original vegetation was forest, this implies planting trees and involves the active management of the land to ensure that the seedlings would survive. If the original vegetation was grassland (in the case of western Qinghai Province, for example), this mostly implies letting the vegetation regenerate and requires much less supervision and active management.

Farmers were compensated for setting aside the land, and in some cases this compensation was higher than the incomes they could have earned from the sale of crops grown on that land. Farmers were compensated eight years for ecological trees (trees which do not generate incomes beyond pruning and felling), five years for economic trees (trees which produce marketable products, such as fruit), and two years for grassland (Qin et al., 2006). For economic trees, this time limit can be rationalized by the fact that after five years the trees can start generating income through the sale of non-timber products (e.g. fruits) and for ecological trees by the fact that after eight years they can generate incomes through pruning, or felling (Li, 2001). In 2007, the program was extended for another cycle because of fears that people would cut the trees if the compensation stopped. In 2015, a new phase of the GfG was initiated, which targets both farmland and wasteland.

The goal of the GfG was to convert approximately 14.67 million ha of farmland to forest (of which 4.4 million ha is situated on land that has a slope greater than 25°) and afforest 17.33 million ha of wasteland by 2010. As can be seen in Figure 5.7, the area of farmland converted increased sharply until 2003, and then slowed down and completely stopped in 2007. The reason for the slowdown was a concern over its impact on food prices, a concern which was later dismissed (Dong et al., 2010).

Over the periods of 1998–2002 and 2003–2007, soil erosion and runoff rates decreased by 45.4 per cent and 18 per cent, respectively, proving that the program was effective in controlling soil erosion (Deng et al., 2012). However, the GfG did not entirely fulfill its targets. By 2012, less than 60 per cent of the original target, about 8.0 million ha of farmland, had been

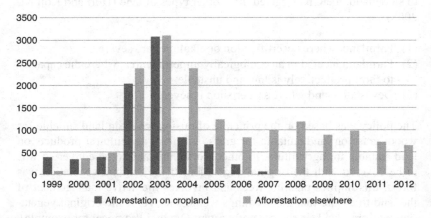

Figure 5.7 GfG reforested area (unit: 1000 hectares)
Source: Chen et al. (2015)

converted, and 16.29 million ha of forests were established through the program (Chen et al., 2015).

Conservation agriculture and conservation tillage

Conservation agriculture aims to achieve sustainable agriculture and improve farmers' livelihoods through the pursuit of three principles: minimal soil disturbance, a permanent soil cover, and crop rotations. On the other hand, conservation tillage refers to a number of methods of land cultivation where the land is not ploughed (no-till farming) and the previous year's plant residue is left on the fields (mulch-till farming). In China, no-till farming amounts to approximately 50 per cent of conservation tillage (Derpsch et al., 2010).

Wind and water erosion, as well as the low soil organic matter (SOM) levels and the consequential decline in productivity, have been the main drivers for the rapid adaptation of conservation agriculture and no-till farming in China (Derpsch et al., 2010). By 2014, over 8 million ha of land were farmed using conservation agriculture approaches (Figure 5.8) (Li et al., 2016). The city of Beijing practices conservation agriculture on more than 85 per cent of its cropland, while the Ministry of Agriculture and the National Development & Reform Commission have prepared a long-term program, approved by the State Council of China, to help spread conservation agriculture practices (Derpsch et al., 2010).

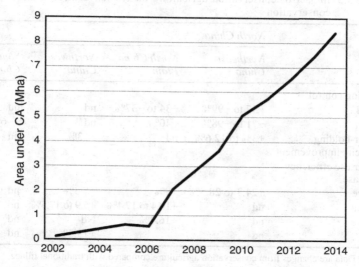

Figure 5.8 Conservation agriculture area in China
Source: Li et al. (2016)

Li et al. (2016) explains that shifting to conservation agriculture could decrease wind erosion and wind-blown sediment transport by at least 30 per cent compared to the erosion processes affecting ploughed land (Table 5.5). In northern China, the conversion of nearly 60 million ha of arable land to conservation agriculture could decrease the annual wind-blown sediment load by 50 per cent, from 6.7 Gt to 3.5 Gt. Shifting to conservation agriculture could also decrease the levels of erosion and the amount of surface runoff by 40 per cent (Table 5.5). By decreasing the losses via runoff and evaporation, the adoption of conservation agriculture would also increase the water-holding capacity and water-use efficiency (WUE) of the soil. Compared to traditional cultivation practices, conservation agriculture can improve the water-holding capacity of soils by 3 per cent and WUE by 10 per cent for most crops and agro-ecoregions (Table 5.5) (Li et al., 2016).

The adoption of conservation agriculture would also control the loss of soil organic carbon (SOC) stocks and increase the amounts of soil microbial biomass carbon, which are important aspects of the soil restoration process. The continuous use of conservation agriculture in China has improved the levels of soil organic matter (SOM) in the topsoil at an annual rate of 0.01 per cent. Such improvement is usually observed only after the long-term (10+ years) utilization of conservation agriculture, with an increase of as much as

Table 5.5 Impact of conservation agriculture on erosion control and moisture conservation

	North China			
	Northeast China	North China Plain	Northwest China	South China
Erosion control				
Wind	−37 to −99%	−34 to −37%	nd	nd
Water	−71 to −98%	−40%	nd	−~60%
Water-holding capacity improvement	+3% to 12.6%	nd	−~3%	nd
Water use efficiency increase				
Maize	+24.3 to 28.5%	+9%	+7.3%	nd
Wheat	nd	+10.4 to 17.4%	+5.9 to 17.5%	nd
Oats	nd	+16.7%	Nd	nd
Peas	nd		+13.3%	nd

Note: Data are changes from conservation agriculture compared with traditional tillage; "nd": no data.

Source: Li et al. (2016)

2.0 g.kg^{-1} in the 0–10 cm layer (Li et al., 2016) (the average content of SOM in topsoil from cropland is 10 g kg^{-1} in China [Fan et al., 2011]). The increase in the concentration of SOC and biotic activity decreases bulk density and improves the pore size distribution and fertility of the soil (Li et al., 2016).

Soil pollution prevention and control measures

Although the authorities were a little slow to realize the magnitude of the soil pollution problem in China, there are now hopeful signs that the government is starting to deal with the problem (He, 2014c). Urgent action is needed, as the heavy metals and metalloids are already entering the food chain. The solutions start with more stringent laws, better technology to treat the soil, and additional funding (Zhao et al., 2014).

Laws about soil pollution

There is a lack of regulations governing soil pollution prevention and control in China, and without laws directly addressing these issues, cases can only be tried as a national tort or criminal offence, which does not ensure environmental remediation. Furthermore, the tort law is ineffective, and criminal laws addressing soil pollution are rarely invoked (Drenguis, 2014).

The government has made some efforts to introduce laws that directly address soil pollution. For example, in 1995, it approved a law (promulgated the following year) on the prevention and control of environmental pollution by solid waste, which also considered soil protection (Mu et al., 2014). However, this law is weakly enforced because the articles are ambiguous, the fines insufficient, and local governments have no incentive to enforce the laws (Drenguis, 2014).

Drenguis (2014) argues that while seemingly well intentioned, the laws are more akin to policy statements than substantive legal requirements. For example, Article 55 of the Solid Waste Law does not define what "relevant provisions" or "specified periods of time" refer to when discussing the management of hazardous waste. By the same token, in Article 32 of the Environmental Protection Law, the steps the government ought to take to dispose of or eliminate hazardous materials have not been specified (Drenguis, 2014: 15). Similarly, Wang Jin, a professor at Peking University and an expert in environmental law, pointed out that Chinese laws look great at first glance but are ineffective when it comes to their implementation (Wang, 2010). The ambiguities resulted in many counties and towns continuing to dispose waste without any treatment (Drenguis, 2014).

More recently, there has been growing attention to the problem of soil pollution, in particular in Hubei Province. In 2016, Wang Jianming, deputy director of Hubei Provincial People's Congress, expressed concerns that China has no specific legislation relating directly to soil protection, which limits the country's soil pollution control and prevention strategies (Zhou and Liu, 2016). As a consequence, the 12th Hubei Provincial People's Congress passed the country's first set of regional laws and guidelines relating to soil pollution prevention. Shortly afterwards, China's 13th Five-Year Plan, published in March 2016, pledged that the country would give priority to cleaning up contaminated soil used in agriculture. It also promised to strengthen its soil pollution monitoring systems and promote new clean-up technologies (Stanway, 2016). According to Yuan Si, vice chairman of the Environment Protection and Resources Conservation Committee (EPRCC) of the National People's Congress (NPC) Standing Committee, in 2017 a bill relating to soil pollution prevention will be introduced to the Standing Committee of the NPC (State Council, 2016b). He also emphasized the need for specific laws directed at soil contamination, because the lack of laws weakens the government's efforts to reduce soil contamination, which, in some parts of China, threatens water and food safety. Laws relating to the prevention of soil contamination will specify the division of responsibilities among government agencies and plans for establishing a survey and control system as well as foster the allocation of larger amounts of monetary assistance, among other things (State Council, 2016b).

Soil Ten Plan

The "Soil Pollution Prevention and Remediation Action Plan" (also called Soil Ten Plan) was issued by the State Council on 31 May 2016 with the aim of comprehensively improving the quality of China's soils by the mid-21st century (State Council, 2016a). The plan aims to address five key tasks: "1) prioritizing the protection of arable lands, 2) controlling the sources of pollution, 3) assessing and managing polluted sites, 4) carrying out soil remediation methods on testing sites, and 5) strengthening the control and maintenance of the soil environment" (China Water Risk, 2014). The action plan lays out ten headline actions split into 35 categories and 231 specific points that should help to achieve the target of making 95 per cent of the currently contaminated land fit to reuse either for agricultural purposes or for new urban development. The action plan lists the following objectives (China Water Risk, 2016):

(1) Key objectives & targets:

- To bring soil contamination under control by 2020, manage soil contamination hazards by 2030 and create a favorable ecological cycle by 2050;
- To ensure that over 90 per cent of the contaminated land can be utilized safely by 2020 and increase this rate to 95 per cent by 2030;
- Local governments need to finalize a detailed work plan and submit it to the group of ministries that developed the plan by 2016;
- To set up national-level soil environmental quality monitoring points and monitoring networks by 2017;
- To set up soil environmental quality monitoring points to cover all the cities and counties by 2020; and
- To establish laws and a regulation system related to soil pollution prevention and control by 2020.

(2) Key pollutants to be monitored:

- Heavy metals: cadmium, mercury, arsenic, lead, and chromium;
- Organic pollutants: PAHs (polycyclic aromatic hydrocarbons) and petroleum hydrocarbons.

(3) Industrial pollution:

- To complete the investigation on the distribution and environmental impacts of contaminated industrial land use by key industries by 2020;

- By 2020, heavy metal emissions from key polluting industries should drop by 10 per cent from the 2013 level;
- To encourage the recycling of electronics, plastic, and packaging waste.

(4) Agricultural pollution:

- To finalize the provincial soil remediation plan and the assessment methods of soil remediation efforts by 2017;
- To finalize the investigation of the total area of contaminated farmlands and the assessment of its impacts on agricultural products by 2018;
- To achieve zero increase of fertilizer and pesticide use in major crops. Effective utilization rates to reach 40 per cent and above. Coverage of fertilizer application based on soil sampling to reach 90 per cent and above by 2020;
- Over 75 per cent of large-scale livestock farms to be equipped with waste management facilities by 2020;
- Irrigation water to comply with farmland irrigation water quality standards.

While the objectives are wide-ranging, many environmental experts and campaigners are disappointed about the lack of details in the document, claiming that it will be challenging to link the ultimate targets and the individual objectives of the plan or to foresee from the specifications alone if the described targets would be reached. Chen Nengchang, a researcher at the Guangdong Institute of Eco-environment and Soil Sciences, said that no details have been provided on the standards that are going to be used to calculate the levels of contamination, what "safe to use" levels refer to, and if the implementation of the plan will be sufficient to achieve the targets (Zhang, 2016).

Environmentalist group Greenpeace also declared that additional legal measures need to be added to China's soil contamination action plan to make it more effective. China will set up a special fund dedicated to combating soil pollution, amounting to about CNY 5 trillion, based on its calculations of the average cost estimates in treating one hectare of land (Miranda, 2016). The action plan requires more financial input from the government, as well as the use of public-private partnerships, but the exact details on how this can be achieved and the private sector's contribution to the plan have yet to be clarified (Zhang, 2016). The government has set aside CNY 450 billion to tackle the multitude of problems with polluted soil (Li, P., 2016). However, the lack of laws and regulations may result in corruption and lead to the mismanagement of the massive investments into soil remediation.

Identifying and monitoring the pollution sources

Identifying and controlling the major sources of pollution is the first step toward addressing the problem (State Council, 2016a). Between 2006 and 2010, the Ministry of Land and Resources (MLR) and the Ministry of Environmental Protection (MEP) carried out the most comprehensive survey of soil pollution in China. A statistical report of the quality of the nation's soil was published in 2014, in which 16 per cent of approximately 10,000 testing sites from 1,500 sampled areas were found to exceed the standards. However, the details of contaminated areas and the associated contaminants were never revealed. As a result, local governments, companies, and the general public are currently unaware of the severity of the country's soil pollution problem. In addition, some academics argue that the survey fails to reflect the real extent of pollution. According to the estimates of Gao Shengda, the editor of the website "China Environmental Remediation", the number of contaminated sites in China ranges between 300,000 and 500,000, which is 30–50 times the number of surveyed sites included in the 2014 report (Zhang, 2016).

In April 2016, hundreds of children at an elite private school in Changzhou, Jiangsu Province, fell ill after the opening of a new campus next to a former chemical plant site (Li, J., 2016). Following that incident, the first map of soil contamination conditions of the country was published by the IPE based on its pollution database, which identified 4,500 companies across 13 polluting industries, including the chemical, mining, and metal industries (Zhang, 2016). The map showed that there were 3,998 state-controlled pollution sources and 502 non-state-controlled ones. In addition, 729 chemical industrial parks were marked on the map (Zhang, 2016). The IPE also produced a map (Figure 5.9) of the level of risk from soil contamination based on the location of 4,500 companies in key industries and over 700 industrial zones.

According to the Soil Ten Plan, new surveys will be conducted to identify the sources of soil pollution and prevent the problem from worsening. By 2018, a new survey will identify the total areas polluted, the distribution of polluted farmland, and the impacts of soil pollution on agricultural products. On the other hand, by 2020, the location of and the environmental risks at key industrial sites will be ascertained. In addition, by 2020, a soil quality control system will be set up throughout China to monitor every region across the country. After that, a survey will be conducted every decade by the Ministry of Environmental Protection along with other government agencies (including the National Development and Reform Commission, the National Health and Family Planning Commission, the Ministry of Industry and Information Technology, the Ministry of Land and Resources,

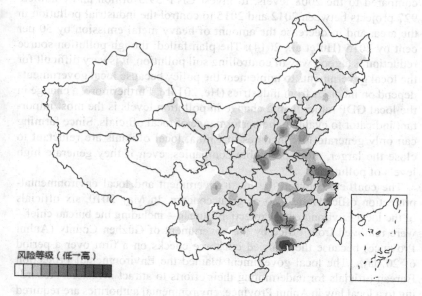

Figure 5.9 Map of soil contamination risk based on the locations of 4,500 companies in key industries and over 700 industrial zones

Source: Zhang (2016)

and the Ministry of Agriculture) to monitor the overall soil quality of China (Soil Ten Plan, 2016). In addition, the action plan includes provisions for better information sharing with the public. A comprehensive database will be established using data collected from the Ministry of Environmental Protection, the Ministry of Land and Resources, and the Ministry of Agriculture, and mobile internet tools will be deployed to receive data updates in real time (State Council, 2016a). However, even though government departments have set goals to build a database and give people access to information about soil conditions, the exact details of the information to be provided have not yet been specified.

Controlling the number of polluting enterprises

China's first officially accepted plan for controlling the heavy metal pollution of a specific area was implemented in the Xiangjiang River basin (Hunan Province) in 2011. Its goals were to halve the number of heavy metal polluting enterprises in the Xiangjiang River basin by 2015 compared to the 2008 levels, to invest CNY 59.5 billion and complete 927 projects between 2012 and 2015 to control the industrial pollution in the area, and to decrease the amount of heavy metal emission by 50 per cent by 2015 (Hu et al., 2014). The plan failed: though pollution source reduction is a good way of controlling soil pollution, it is very difficult for the local governments to implement the policy because local governments depend on incomes from industries (He, 2014b). Furthermore, a change in the local GDP rather than a change in pollution levels is the most important indicator to evaluate the performance of local officials. Since farming can only generate low incomes in China, local officials are reluctant to close the larger, more profitable companies, even if they generate high levels of pollution.

The conflicts between the local government and local environmental-protection officials are also of great concern. In May 2010, six officials of the local Environmental Protection Bureau – including the bureau chief – were removed from office by the government of Guzhen County (Anhui Province) because they carried out three checks on a firm over a period of 20 days. The local government blamed the Environmental Protection Bureau officials for undermining their efforts to attract investors. According to a local law in Anhui Province, environmental authorities are required to obtain a permission before conducting checks, a policy that provides protection against unexpected checks to the largest energy consumers and polluters (Wang, 2010).

Similarly, Wong (2013) reports how in Hengyang (Hunan Province) a large heap of industrial waste has ruined farmlands and caused outraged comments from villagers on the internet. However, the factories are closely tied to government officials, and in the eyes of Hunan officials, the industries surrounding Hengyang are fundamental to maintaining Hunan's leading role in non-ferrous metal production. The farmers do not expect to see improvements (Wong, 2013).

The Soil Ten Plan has set goals to strengthen the regulation on pollution sources. According to the plan, the government will

> strictly implement the heavy metal pollutant emission standards [. . .]; take stronger measures for the supervision and inspection of enterprises; and the [. . .] enterprises that do not meet [the] standards after [they] have been updated will be suspended or permanently stopped.
> (Soil Ten Plan, 2016: 21)

Considering the current situation of weak laws and enforcements, it is doubtful these goals will be fulfilled.

Reclassification of soil use

In the Soil Ten Plan, agricultural soils are classified into three categories to maintain the safety of crops and livestock products: (1) non-contaminated and slightly contaminated soils, whose protection will be given priority, (2) mildly and moderately contaminated soils, which will be treated and classified as safe to use, and (3) severely contaminated soils, which will be brought under strict control (State Council, 2016a). By the end of 2017,

> the technical guidelines for the categorization of the environmental quality of arable land will be released. By the end of 2020, arable land and agricultural products shall be concurrently monitored and evaluated based on a detailed survey of soil contamination, and such categorization will be promoted nationwide, starting with the pilot projects.
>
> (Soil Ten Plan, 2016: 9)

While the plan aims to ensure a safe environment for agricultural production by categorizing agricultural land, issues of the reclassification of land go beyond agriculture.

In cities, many former industrial sites have been abandoned because of contamination concerns. Between 2001 and 2009, at least 98,000 industrial plants were closed and relocated across the country. Many of the industrial plants were highly polluting state-owned factories that were built during the Great Leap Forward (Drenguis, 2014). These former industrial zones have been reclassified for residential use, which poses health risks to both construction workers and the future residents. But these health hazards of pollution are not limited to industrial land. Many real estate developers are hoping for the reclassification of contaminated farmlands so they can be used for non-agricultural purposes (He, 2014a). Although Chinese law requires the soil to be analyzed for contaminants before large construction projects commence, this requirement is generally ignored. One widely publicized case happened in 2007 in Wuhan (Hebei Province) after a former pesticide factory site was repurposed for residential use. Construction work was suspended after a worker suffered serious chemical poisoning. Following the incident, the government was compelled to refund the purchase price of the building site, pay a CNY 130 million reimbursement to the development company, and spend nearly CNY 300 million to clean up the poisonous materials from the area (He, 2014a).

Promoting applicable technologies to reduce soil pollutants

Soil remediation projects are only beginning to be implemented. Liu Yangsheng, the secretary-general of the Heavy Metals and Environmental Remediation Committee of China's Environmental Protection Industry Association, expressed his fear that the rehabilitation of heavy metal polluted soil will be a long and slow process due to the ill-defined evaluation standards, rudimentary technology, and lack of funding. He also pointed out that costly techniques are unlikely to be widely adopted due to the magnitude of heavy metal contamination in the country. Also, overseas rehabilitation techniques that may be effective for small areas are not applicable to the vast polluted areas in China (He, 2014a). According to the Soil Ten Plan, 200 pilot projects will be launched to test soil pollution treatment and remediation technologies by the end of 2020. Once the pilot projects are completed, the results will be evaluated, and the best technologies will be selected (Drenguis, 2014). Both chemical and biological approaches may be used.

Chemical approaches

In China, the most commonly used chemical strategy to reduce the amounts of heavy metals absorbed by plants is liming. Liming is the application of calcium- and magnesium-rich materials which neutralize soil acidity and increase the activity of soil bacteria (Tyler and Olsson, 2001). Liming also manipulates the phytoavailability of metals, reducing the amount of metal that is taken up by the plant (Zhao et al., 2014). The technique of liming acidic soils should be applied particularly on lands heavily polluted by high-risk contaminants, such as Cd and Pb. When lime is applied to the soil, the heavy metal pollutants will oxidize, which lessens the chances of the plant roots absorbing them (Stanway, 2014). There are a variety of liming materials on the market with different reaction rates, acid-neutralizing capacities, and costs. The application of several rounds of liming material over successive crop seasons may increase the pH to the desired level, but its over-application may also result in harm to plant life (Zhao et al., 2014).

Biological approaches

There are also biological methods for soil remediation. For example, the metal pollutants can be detoxified using microorganisms to transform their valences, precipitate chemicals outside of the cells, or enzymatically reduce metals by metabolic processes, rather than absorb them. An alternative method is phytoremediation: the planting of specific plants such as willows, birches, and leguminous plants, which absorb and remove the pollutants from the soil. The plants can then be harvested, processed, and disposed of. Besides being cheaper than physicochemical procedures, this approach also has the advantage of permanently removing the pollutants from the soil. However, for such methods to be applicable to the vast areas of polluted agricultural soils in China, they need to be both efficient and cost-effective, because farmers can neither afford to invest in expensive soil remediation techniques nor suspend their farming activities for years (Lone et al., 2008). As Chen Nengchang, a soil remediation specialist at the Guangdong Institute of Eco-Environment and Soil Sciences, explains, cultivating non-food grains would clean the soil over time. However, producing sufficient grain for its large and growing population is of prime concern to the government, so shifting to the production of non-food grains is only proposed for the more heavily polluted soils (He, 2014a).

According to He (2014a), the Foshan Jinkuizi Plant Nutrition Company has pioneered a technique for soil remediation with the specific purpose of rehabilitating China's heavy metal-contaminated soils. The company has developed a microorganism capable of changing the ionic property of heavy metals in the soil, thus deactivating the contaminants. The company argues that their technique is cost-efficient, easy to use, and is already available in commercial form, and its application does not create secondary pollutants. In another possible breakthrough, the Guangdong Geoanalysis Research Center has developed a new material, Mont-SH6, which it claims is capable of absorbing heavy metal pollutants such as lead, cadmium, zinc, mercury, and copper. According to Liu Wenhua, chief engineer at the research center, the new product is capable of reducing the cadmium levels of the soil by more than 90 per cent, and the material's cost of production is low: the remediation process for 0.6 ha of cadmium-polluted rice fields would cost about CNY 33,000. However, according to Liu, mass production could reduce these costs to CNY 2,200–3,300 (He, 2014a).

Although experiments with microorganisms and plants that are capable of absorbing soil pollutants are promising, it is questionable how effective they will be, given the extent of the problem (Stanway, 2014). Also, there isn't a universal solution for the country's polluted soils. For example, a species of Indian mustard has been shown to be effective in absorbing selenium, and Chinese ferns can accumulate arsenic, but they have little impact on other pollutants.

Challenges

The central government has shown a strong determination to address China's issues of soil pollution; however, significant results are yet to be seen (Kong, 2015). Disagreements between local governments are one reason for the delay of a nationwide policy. Unlike air and water pollution, soil pollution can be more effectively tackled with regional strategies than through an overarching national approach. The geological properties of soil differ from region to region, and local authorities must figure out the most suitable strategies for the local conditions. For instance, some areas might naturally have higher concentrations of metals, in which case a better way to mitigate risk is to ensure the land is used appropriately, rather than through soil remediation. Moreover, unlike air and water, soil does not travel, which means that provincial governments can manage their own soil without the need for cross-border coordination. Also, the heavy reliance of soil management policies on researchers, laboratories, and equipment can most easily be met by provincial-level governments (Kong, 2015).

Indeed, some scholars argued that regionally implemented policies can more efficiently meet the needs of China's cities and provinces, compared to top-down political directives. Shanghai was the first local government to establish its own soil policy. The city developed its clean soil standards in 2007 in the run-up to the World Expo 2010. This set of standards has since become a valuable reference for other cities, indicating that the central government should provide stronger incentives to selected provincial governments to develop their own strategies and become pioneers in soil protection policies. By focusing investment on a couple of selected provinces, relevant skills and mechanisms can be developed more efficiently (Kong, 2015).

Apart from the difficulty in implementing uniform policies across local governments, experts in the field suggest that technical barriers have been a major hindrance for provincial governments. There are various contaminants, including heavy metals like cadmium or lead, volatile organic compounds (VOCs) such as benzene, persistent organic pollutants (POPs) coming from different chemicals and pesticides, and waste left by fossil fuel combustion. All these pollutants require different techniques to be removed from the soil. Besides, many local institutions are confused about clean soil standards, the right technology for soil inspection and treatment, and management strategies for vast areas of land. Local governments may need more guidance from the central government to overcome such barriers (Kong, 2015).

Besides the technological and legislative challenges, the biggest difficulty is the funding of soil remediation projects. The costs of cleaning up the polluted land are indeed staggering. In 2015, the central government assigned a budget of CNY 2.8 billion for anti-pollution programs across 30 prefecture-level cities, but experts claim this amount is far from sufficient. According to Lan Hong, a professor at Renmin University, "even with cheap restoration methods, it would take CNY 300,000 per hectare of land polluted by heavy metals, which means at least CNY 6 trillion is needed"

(Deng and Leng, 2016). On the other hand, the Jiangsu Institute of Environmental Industry estimated that China's soil remediation industry is a market that could reach CNY 757 billion between 2014 and 2020, financed almost entirely by government subsidies (He, 2014a). Zhuang Guotai, the head of the Ministry of Environmental Protection's Department of Nature and Ecology Conservation, estimated that the total cleanup costs could eventually reach CNY 11 trillion. Although there are some available remediation techniques, the country needs more low-cost technologies to tackle a problem of this magnitude (Stanway, 2014).

While investors can impose a fee for cleaned wastewater, it is difficult to do so for clean soil, so there is the potential for only a small cost recovery from soil rehabilitation. The involvement of developers who are interested to clean up polluted urban sites could mean a possible funding solution, but this possibility has had limited results so far (Hornby, 2015). This raises the problem of obtaining private funds for soil rehabilitation.

Wangxia Hui, one of the MEP directors, pointed out that until now the responsibility of the parties joining forces against soil pollution has not been clarified. Soil pollution prevention and control is one of the responsibilities of many different government departments, including environmental protection, development and reform, science and technology, finance, land, housing construction, and agriculture, but there has not yet been a good mechanism for all these parties to work together. For example, when preparing an urban and rural development plan, most local planning authorities do not give soil quality sufficient consideration. Finally, public participation in soil protection is limited due to the lack of appropriate mechanisms for the public to know the extent of soil pollution (Guo and Dai, 2016).

Conclusions

Soil degradation and soil pollution are the outcome of various natural factors and human activities that result from people's inadequate use of land resources and the "grow first, clean up later" attitude prevalent in China (Currell, 2013). This attitude is proving very expensive now that soil degradation and pollution have reached critical levels. Chinese people are concerned about the quality of the food, and China is forced to import food from other countries. Efforts to restore and clean up the soil are underway, but it is an expensive and time-consuming process.

To address soil degradation, the government has undertaken a number of measures, in particular reforestation and vegetation restoration programs in the most degraded – and least agriculturally productive – areas. However, soil erosion in China covers very large areas with various types of climates, landforms, soils, and vegetation, with significant variations in natural conditions, social conditions, and economic activities. For this reason, measures to prevent, control and fix soil degradation should be adapted to the regional conditions (Yin et al., 2005). Regrettably, the government tends to promote nationwide policies with little regard to regional anomalies and local characteristic, which result in the relative failure of some of those policies (for example, reforestation in the Loess Plateau).

Soil pollution is different from soil degradation in that it is more difficult to identify, its pollution is directly related to economic activities (whether the excessive use of pesticides or industrial emissions), and it is more expensive to remediate. China's rapid economic growth and disregard for its environmental problems, partly originating from China's desire to put an end to poverty and partly on the assumption that the inflicted damage could be repaired later at a relatively cheap cost, has resulted in about one-fifth of the country's cropland already being severely contaminated. The Chinese government has finally decided that the "clean up later" period has arrived, and China's State Council has recently instructed that over 90 per cent of the contaminated land should be safe to use by 2020, and 95 per cent by 2030, as part of the Soil Ten Plan.

A further problem which prevents soil pollution from being easily tackled is that on the one hand, soil pollution is a direct result of air emissions from manufacturing industries, so emissions have to be curbed by regulating and, if necessary, fining or closing these industries. On the other hand, these same manufacturing industries provide the bulk of the taxation to the local governments, so a threat of leaving the area if regulated or fined may stop the local governments from acting. Furthermore, if the companies actually do close, the government may be starved of the funds needed to clean up the pollution, and the companies may just open in other provinces with less stringent standards. These are clear contradictions that may prevent a successful outcome of the government's soil rehabilitation efforts. Nevertheless, the regulations reflect the country's determination to finally address its soil pollution problems. If the central government provides enough financial support and establishes and enforces concomitant laws, the goals would likely be achieved (Deng and Leng, 2016).

Bibliography

Cao, S. (2008). Why large-scale afforestation efforts in China have failed to solve the desertification problem. *Environmental Science & Technology, 42*(6), 1826–1831.
Cao, S., Chen, L., Shankman, D., Wang, C., Wang, X., & Zhang, H. (2011). Excessive reliance on afforestation in China's arid and semi-arid regions: Lessons in ecological restoration. *Earth-Science Reviews, 104*(4), 240–245.

Cao, S. X., Tian, T., Chen, L., Dong, X. B., Yu, X. X., & Wang, G. S. (2010). Damage caused to the environment by reforestation policies in arid and semi-arid areas of China. *Ambio*, *39*, 279–283. DOI: 10.1007/s13280–010–0038-z

Chen, C., König, H. J., Matzdorf, B., & Zhen, L. (2015). The institutional challenges of Payment for Ecosystem Service Program in China: A review of the effectiveness and implementation of Sloping Land Conversion Program. *Sustainability*, *7*(5), 5564–5591.

Chen, E. (November, 2013). The Loess Plateau of China and its soil erosion problems. Retrieved from https://geog5loessplateau.wordpress.com/

China Water Risk. (2014). Soil pollution standards & proposed law. Retrieved 15 December 2016 from http://chinawaterrisk.org/notices/new-soil-pollution-standards/

China Water Risk. (2016). New 'Soil Ten Plan' to safeguard China's food safety & healthy living environment. Retrieved 15 December 2016 from http://chinawaterrisk.org/notices/new-soil-ten-plan-to-safeguard-chinas-food-safety-healthy-living-environment/

Currell, M. (December, 2013). Shanghai's 'airpocalypse': Can China fix its deadly pollution? Retrieved 15 December 2016 from http://theconversation.com/shanghais-airpocalypse-can-china-fix-its-deadly-pollution-21275

Delang, C. O. (2016a). *China's Water Pollution Problems*. London: Routledge.

Delang, C. O. (2016b). *China's Air Pollution Problems*. London: Routledge.

Delang, C. O., & Wang, W. (2013). Chinese forest policy reforms after 1998: The case of the Natural Forest Protection Program and the Slope Land Conversion Program. *International Forestry Review*, *15*(3), 290–304.

Delang, C. O., & Yuan, Z. (2015). *China's Grain for Green Program*. Cham: Springer International Publishing.

Démurger, S., Fournier, M., & Shen, G. Z. (2005). Forest Protection Policies: National guidelines and their local implementation in northern Sichuan. Retrieved 15 December 2016 from https://chinaperspectives.revues.org/481

Deng, L., Shangguan, Z. P., & Li, R. (2012). Effects of the grain-for-green program on soil erosion in China. *International Journal of Sediment Research*, *27*(1), 131–138.

Deng, X. C., & Leng, S. M. (June, 2016). China determined to clean up 90% of polluted arable land by 2020. *Global Times*. Retrieved 15 December 2016 from www.globaltimes.cn/content/986279.shtml

Derpsch, R., Friedrich, T., Kassam, A., & Li, H. (2010). Current status of adoption of no-till farming in the world and some of its main benefits. *International Journal of Agricultural and Biological Engineering*, *3*(1), 1–25.

Dong, J., Liu, J., & Shi, W. (2010). China's Slope Land Conversion Program at the beginning of 21st century and its habitat suitability in typical region of Loess Plateau. *Journal of Resources and Ecology*, *1*(1), 36–44.

Drenguis, D. D. (2014). Reap what you sow: Soil pollution remediation reform in China. *Pacific Rim Law & Policy Journal Association*, *23*, 171.

Duan, Z., Xiao, H., Li, X., Dong, Z., & Wang, G. (2004). Evolution of soil properties on stabilized sands in the Tengger Desert, China. *Geomorphology*, *59*(1), 237–246.

Economy, E. C. (January, 2003). China's Environmental Challenge: Political, Social and Economic Implications. Council on Foreign Relations. Testimony before the Congressional Executive Commission on China Roundtable on the Environment. January 27, 2003. Retrieved 15 December 2016 from www.cfr.org/china/chinas-environmental-challenge-political-social-economic-implications/p5573

Fan, M. S., Shen, J. B., Yuan, L. X., Jiang, R. F., Chen, X. P., Davies, W. J., & Zhang, F. (2011). Improving crop productivity and resource use efficiency to ensure food security and environmental quality in China. *Journal of Experimental Botany, 2011*, 1–12.

FAO. (2016). *Conversation Agriculture*. Rome: Food and Agriculture Organisation of the United Nations. Retrieved from www.fao.org/ag/ca/

Feng, Q., Ma, H., Jiang, X. M., Wang, X., & Cao, S. X. (2015). What has caused desertification in China? Nature. *Scientific Reports, 5*. Article ID 15998. Retrieved from www.nature.com/articles/srep15998

Gates, J., Zhang, L., Dr., Xingmin, M., & Scanlon, B. (2016). *Impact of Soil Conservation Practices on Water Resources in the Loess Plateau, China*. Austin: Bureau of Economic Geology, University of Texas. Retrieved 15 December 2016 from www.beg.utexas.edu/cswr/loess.html

Guo, X., & Dai, Y. (May, 2016). Soil pollution control what difficulties children? Expert: Weak infrastructure, backward legislation, unclear responsibilities. Retrieved 15 December 2016 from www.top-news.top/news-12153368.html

He, G. (July, 2014a). The soil pollution crisis in China: A cleanup presents daunting challenge. *Environment 360*. Retrieved 15 December 2016 from http://e360.yale.edu/feature/the_soil_pollution_crisis_in_china_a_cleanup_presents_daunting_challenge/2786/

He, G. (July, 2014b). In China's heartland, a toxic trail leads from factories to fields to food. *Environment 360*. Retrieved 15 December 2016 from http://e360.yale.edu/feature/chinas_toxic_trail_leads_from_factories_to_food/2784/

He, G. (July, 2014c). China's dirty pollution secret: The boom poisoned its soil and crops. *Environment 360*. Retrieved 15 December 2016 from http://e360.yale.edu/feature/chinas_dirty_pollution_secret_the_boom_poisoned_its_soil_and_crops/2782/

He, J., & Sikor, T. (2015). Notions of justice in payments for ecosystem services: Insights from China's Sloping Land Conversion Program in Yunnan Province. *Land Use Policy, 43*, 207–216.

Hori, S., & Kojima, K. (2008). The impact of the Sloping Land Conversion Program on rural area in China: A case study in Yulin district. *Japan Society of Tropical Ecology Tropics, 17*(2), 169–184.

Hornby, L. (September, 2015). Chinese environment: Ground operation. *Financial Times*. Retrieved 15 December 2016 from www.ft.com/content/d096f594-4be0-11e5-b558-8a9722977189

Hu, H., Jin, Q., & Kavan, P. (2014). A study of heavy metal pollution in China: Current status, pollution-control policies and countermeasures. *Sustainability, 6*, 5820–5838. DOI:10.3390/su6095820

Iversen, W. (May, 2016). President Xi emphasizes importance of forest protection during visit to Heilongjiang. *Canada Wood Today*. Retrieved 15 December 2016 from http://canadawood.org/blog/president-xi-emphasizes-importance-of-forest-protection-during-visit-to-heilongjiang/

Kong, A. (May, 2015). No quick fix for China's polluted soil. *South China Morning Post*. Retrieved 15 December 2016 from www.scmp.com/comment/insight-opinion/article/1783358/no-quick-fix-chinas-polluted-soil

LADA. (October, 2010). *China National Level Report of Land Degradation Assessment in Drylands*. Prepared by: LADA Project Team, P. R. China. Rome: FAO.

Li, H. W., He, J., Bharucha, Z. P., Lal, R., & Pretty, J. (2016). Improving China's food and environmental security with conservation agriculture. *International Journal of Agricultural Sustainability, 14*(4), 377–391. DOI: 10.1080/14735903.2016.1170330

Li, J. (April, 2016). Are you at risk from China's polluted soil? Check this map. *South China Morning Post*. Retrieved 15 December 2016 from www.scmp.com/news/china/policies-politics/article/1940108/are-you-risk-chinas-polluted-soil-check-map

Li, P. (June, 2016). CBBC Insights: Environment-China issues soil pollution act to complement existing air and water policies. *China British Business Council*. Retrieved 15 December 2016 from www.cbbc.org/news/cbbc-insights-environment-china-issues-soil-pollut/

Li, Y. C. (2001). Push the conversion of cropland to forest and grassland program to a new stage. *Green China, 2001*(9), 3–11 (in Chinese).

Li, Y. S. (1997). Relation between control in Loess Plateau and no-flow in the Yellow River. *Bulletin of Soil and Water Conservation, 17*(6), 41–45 (in Chinese).

Liu, C., & Wu, B. (2010). 'Grain for green program' in China: Policy making and implementation? The University of Nottingham. *Policy Briefing Series*, (60). Retrieved 15 December 2016 from www.nottingham.ac.uk/cpi/documents/briefings/briefing-60-reforestation.pdf

Liu, Z., & Lan, J. (2015). The Sloping Land Conversion Program in China: Effect on the livelihood diversification of rural households. *World Development, 70*, 147–161. Retrieved from http://dx.doi.org/10.1016/j.worlddev.2015.01.004

Lone, M. L., He, Z. L., Stoffella, P. J., & Yang, X. E. (2008). Phytoremediation of heavy metal polluted soils and water: Progresses and perspectives. *Journal of Zhejiang University Science B, 9*(3), 210–220. Retrieved 15 December 2016 from www.ncbi.nlm.nih.gov/pmc/articles/PMC2266886/

Lu, W. M., Landell-Mills, N., Liu, J. L., Xu, J. T., & Liu, C. (2002). *Getting the Private Sector to Work for the Public Good: Instruments for Sustainable Private Sector Forestry in China*. London: International Institute for Environment and Development.

Luoma, J. R. (January, 2012). China's reforestation programs: Big success or just an illusion? *Environment 360*. Retrieved 15 December 2016 from http://e360.yale.edu/feature/chinas_reforestation_programs_big_success_or_just_an_illusion/2484/

Miranda, E. (June, 2016). Greenpeace to China: Give soil pollution action plan 'teeth', add legal measures. *Yibada*. Retrieved 15 December 2016 from http://en.yibada.com/articles/128323/20160602/greenpeace-to-china-give-soil-pollution-action-plan-teeth-add-legal-measures.htm#ixzz4HrhhUfFX

140   *Solutions to soil degradation and pollution*

Mu, Z. L., Bu, S. C., & Xue, B. (2014). Environmental legislation in China: Achievements, challenges and trends. *Sustainability, 6,* 8967–8979. DOI: 10.3390/su6128967

MWR. (July, 2016). *Soil and Water Conservation in China.* Beijing: Ministry of Water Resources. Retrieved 15 December 2016 from www.tnmc-is.org/wp-content/uploads/2016/07/6.SOIL%20AND%20WATER%20CONSERVATION%20IN%20CHINA.pdf

Qin, J. M., An, M. Z., Shi, C. F., & Yang, H. (2006). Compensating standard and time of converting cropland to forestry. *Inner Mongolia Forestry Investigation and Design, 29*(1), 20–24 (in Chinese).

Ren, G. P., Young, S. S., Wang, L., Wang, W., Long, Y. C., Wu, R., Li, J., Zhu, J., & Yu, D. W. (2015). Effectiveness of China's National Forest Protection Program and nature reserves. *Conservation Biology, 29*(5), 1368–1377. DOI: 10.1111/cobi.12561

Schmitz, P. M., Mal, P., & Hesse, J. W. (2015). *The Importance of Conservation Tillage as a Contribution to Sustainable Agriculture: A Special Case of Soil Erosion.* Giessen, Germany: Institut für Agribusiness. Retrieved 15 December 2016 from http://agribusiness.de/images/stories/Forschung/Agribusiness_Forschung_33_Conservation_Tillage.pdf

Soil Ten Plan. (2016). Action Plan for Prevention and Control of Soil Pollution. Danish Soil Partnership. Retrieved 15 December 2016 from http://danishsoil.org/media/test_sites/uploads/Soil%20Ten%20Plan.pdf

Stanway, D. (September, 2014). FACTBOX-solutions to China's soil contamination crisis. *Reuters.* Retrieved from http://uk.reuters.com/article/china-pollution-technology-idUKL3N0QZ2CL20140916

Stanway, D. (May, 2016). China releases new action plan to tackle soil pollution. *Reuters.* Retrieved from www.reuters.com/article/us-china-environment-soil-idUSKCN0YM0YO

State Council. (May, 2016a). *Efforts to Prevent and Remedy Soil Pollution.* Beijing: The State Council of the People's Republic of China. Retrieved 15 December 2016 from http://english.gov.cn/policies/latest_releases/2016/05/31/content_281475361737430.htm

State Council. (March, 2016b). *China Working on Law to Tackle Soil Pollution.* Beijing: The State Council of People's Republic of China. Retrieved 15 December 2016 from http://english.gov.cn/news/top_news/2016/03/10/content_281475304770375.htm

Sun, X. F., Canby, K., & Liu, L. J. (March, 2016). China's Logging Ban in Natural Forests: Impacts of Extended Policy at Home and Abroad. Forest Trends Information Brief. Retrieved 15 December 2016 from www.forest-trends.org/documents/files/doc_5145.pdf

Tyler, G., & Olsson, T. (2001). Plant uptake of major and minor mineral elements as influenced by soil acidity and liming. *Plant and Soil, 230*(2), 307–321.

Wang, J. (September, 2010). China's green laws are useless. *China Dialogue.* Retrieved 15 December 2016 from www.chinadialogue.net/article/show/single/en/3831

Wong, E. (December, 2013). Pollution rising, Chinese fear for soil and food. *New York Times.* Retrieved 15 December 2016 from www.nytimes.com/2013/12/31/world/asia/good-earth-no-more-soil-pollution-plagues-chinese-countryside.html?_r=0

World Bank. (April, 2003). *Loess Plateau Watershed Rehabilitation Project*. New York: The World Bank. Retrieved 15 December 2016 from http://worldbank.mrooms.net/file.php/347/docs/LoessPlateau_ICR-2003.pdf

Wu, Y. (May, 2015). Washing away soil erosion worries. *Shanghai Daily*. Retrieved 15 December 2016 from www.shanghaidaily.com/feature/news-feature/Washing-away-soil-erosion-worries/shdaily.shtml

Xu, X. Z., Zhang, H. W., & Zhang, O. Y. (2004). Development of check-dam systems in gullies on the Loess Plateau, China. *Environmental Science & Policy*, 7(2), 79–86.

Xu, X. Z., Li, M. J., Liu, B., Kuang, S. F., & Xu, S. G. (2012). Quantifying the effects of conservation practices on soil, water, and nutrients in the Loess Mesa Ravine Region of the Loess Plateau, China. *Environmental Management*, 49(5), 1092–1101. DOI: 10.1007/s00267-012-9835-4

Yin, R. S., Xu, J. T., Li, Z., & Liu, C. (2005). China's ecological rehabilitation: The unprecedented efforts and dramatic impacts of reforestation and slope protection in Western China. *China Environment Series*, 6, 17–32.

Zhang, C. (June, 2016). Lack of data, openness could obstruct soil clean up. *Earth Journalism Network*. Retrieved from http://earthjournalism.net/stories/lack-of-data-openness-could-obstruct-soil-clean-up

Zhao, F. J., Ma, Y. B., Zhu, Y. G., Tang, Z., & McGrath, S. P. (2014). Soil contamination in China: Current status and mitigation strategies. American Chemical Society. *Environmental Science & Technology*, 49(2), 750–759.

Zhao, S. C. (2015). Protect all natural forest strictly. State Forest Administration. Retrieved from www.forestry.gov.cn/main/195/content-742128.html (in Chinese).

Zheng, D. (2003). Wind erosion and land degradation in Inner Mongolia, China. The International Society for Agricultural Meteorology. Retrieved 15 December 2016 from www.agrometeorology.org/topics/needs-for-agrometeorological-solutions-to-farming-problems/wind-erosion-and-land-degradation-in-inner-mongolia-china

Zhou, L., & Liu, K. (February, 2016). China's first soil pollution prevention regulations introduced. *China Daily*. Retrieved 15 December 2016 from www.chinadaily.com.cn/china/2016-02/01/content_23348053.htm

Zhou, W. (August, 2011). Huge stockpiles of toxic waste in 12 provinces. *China Daily*. Retrieved 15 December 2016 from www.chinadaily.com.cn/cndy/2011-08/31/content_13224360.htm

Index

Italic page references indicate figures or tables.

control measures 124–35; promoting applicable technologies to reduce 132–3; Soil Ten Plan 126–31, 130; standards 9–12; from urbanization 57–62

pollution, water 1

polychlorinated biphenyl 91

population and urbanization 31

potassium 50, 70

prevention and control measures, land degradation *see* solutions

Qinghai Province 41; soil nutrient deficiency in 71

Rao, E. 19, 20, 23

reclassification of soil use 131

recycling 60

reforestation 1, 135–6; effectiveness of 116; Grain for Green program, 5, 8, 119–22; Natural Forest Protection Program (NFPP) 117–19; of dryland areas 3, 111–16; of wasteland areas 3

Ren, G. P. 118

reservoirs 88–90

rice: cancer villages and 100; heavy metal contamination of 93–4; production 16–17, 79–81

road construction 61–2

salinization, soil 71–2, *73*

sandification 77–8

sandstorms and dust 84–5

Sanmenxia Reservoir 89

sedimentation, reservoir 88–90

Shaanxi Province 20, 24, 25, 37; coal in 54; reservoirs in 89

Shandong Province 8, 45, 49; cancer villages 99

Shanxi Province 24, 25, 37, 49

Shen-Ha Highway 62

Shenmuwaluo Reservoir 89

shrublands 20

Sichuan Province 20, 24, 25

silt filling in dams 88–90

soil: acidification 73–4; cadmium in 9, 42–4; effective cation exchange capacity (ECEC) 81–2; geographic distribution of heavy metals in 43–5; lead in 44; nutrients 70–1;

quality 8–9; resources in China 4–8; salinization 71–2, *73*; use reclassification 131; vital role of 4

soil degradation 1–2, 31–2; acidification and 73–4; amount of 18–19; causes of 26, 32–42; damages to grassland with reduced livestock products 81–3; desertification and 75–8; direct impacts of 70–8; distribution of 19–26; due to agricultural and livelihood activities 39–42; due to permafrost 36; due to water erosion 36–9; due to wind erosion 34–5; erosion rates 19–20; general conditions of 33–9; impact on production processes 78–83, 101; impacts on ecosystem services 83–90; indirect impacts of 78–90; prevention and control measures 109–24; salinization and 71–2, *73*; significance of impacts of 69; soil nutrients loss due to 70–1; standards 17, *18*; types and severity of 33–4

soil organic carbon (SOC) 70–1, 123–4

soil pollution: from agricultural activities 46–54; causes of 42–62, 63; controlling the number of polluting enterprises and 129–30; difficulty in monitoring 26; geographic distribution of 12–17; identifying and monitoring sources of 128–9; impacts of 69, 90–100; from industrial activities 54–62; lack of awareness of 1–2; laws 124–5; localized 12–13; prevention and control measures 124–35; promoting applicable technologies to reduce 132–3; Soil Ten Plan 126–31; standards 9–12; from urbanization 57–62

Soil Ten Plan 126–31

solutions 108–9; conservation agriculture and conservation tillage 122–4; controlling the number of polluting enterprises 129–30; government policy challenges 133–5; Grain for Green (GfG) program 5, 8, 119–22; identifying and monitoring pollution sources 128–9; land degradation prevention